15-minute foc...
Brief Counseling
Techniques that W...

MW00425252

BEHAVIORAL
THREAT ASSESSMENT
AND MANAGEMENT
FOR K-12 SCHOOLS

Funding to help underwrite the development of
the *15-Minute Focus* series has been generously provided by:

Maclellan Family Foundations

We partner with the courageous
to change the world.

PASTORAL INSTITUTE

SARAH T. BUTLER
CHILDREN'S CENTER
COLUMBUS, GEORGIA

The Sarah T. Butler Children's Center at the Pastoral Institute of Columbus, Georgia is dedicated to the mental health and well-being of children ages 1-18. This center provides comprehensive services that span psychological testing, intervention, therapy groups, and counseling. In all our activities we seek to inspire growth through faith, hope, and love.

NATIONAL CENTER for
YOUTH ISSUES

P.O. Box 22185
Chattanooga, TN 37422-2185
423.899.5714 • 866.318.6294
fax: 423.899.4547 • www.ncyi.org

Print ISBN: 9781953945457
E-book ISBN: 9781953945501
Library of Congress Control Number: 2021906820
© 2021 National Center for Youth Issues, Chattanooga, TN
All rights reserved.
Written by: Dr. Melissa A. Louvar Reeves
Published by National Center for Youth Issues
Printed in the U.S.A. • October 2022

Third party links are accurate at the time of publication, but may change over time.

The information in this book is designed to provide helpful information on the subjects discussed and is not intended to be used, nor should it be used, to diagnose or treat any mental health or medical condition. For diagnosis or treatment of any mental health or medical issue, consult a licensed counselor, psychologist, or physician. The publisher and author are not responsible for any specific mental or physical health needs that may require medical supervision, and are not liable for any damages or negative consequences from any treatment, action, application, or preparation, to any person reading or following the information in this book. References are provided for informational purposes only and do not constitute endorsement of any websites or other sources.

Contents

INTRODUCTION 3

CHAPTER 1

What is Behavioral Threat Assessment and Management (BTAM)?............7

CHAPTER 2

BTAM Legal and Ethical Considerations...19

CHAPTER 3

Foundations to Effective Threat Assessment and Management 27

CHAPTER 4

Establish the Multi-Disciplinary Team.. 35

CHAPTER 5

Identification and Reporting of Concerns..51

CHAPTER 6

Establish BTAM Assessment Procedures 59

CHAPTER 7

Developing Risk Management Options 81

CHAPTER 8

Role of Administrators & Collaboration with SROs and School Mental
Health Professionals...95

CHAPTER 9

Role of School Mental Health Professionals 105

CHAPTER 10

Community Partnerships and Transitioning to the Adult Community 113

CONCLUDING THOUGHTS 117

RESOURCES AND TRAINING 118

Appendix A 121

Appendix B 123

References.. 125

Endnotes.. 127

See page 117 for information about Downloadable Resources.

Introduction

Taylor is so excited to be back at school! She can feel the excitement in the air as there is some sense of hope that normalcy will return after months of alternating between in-person and virtual instruction. She senses an energy that she has not felt in months as excitement builds for the basketball game on Friday. But there is one exception. Jordan is typically a quiet yet friendly student, well-liked by others. While not the most popular, Jordan is certainly not considered an outcast. Lately, Jordan has been posting concerning social media posts that show increased anger and frustration with the division and fighting going on in our country, increased discontent with school, and themes of hopelessness and helplessness that things will never get back to normal. Today, Jordan is making little eye contact. Taylor tries to engage Jordan in a conversation about the basketball game and asks if Jordan will be going. Jordan's reply is, "I'm thinking about it, but there's stuff I need to take care of. People need to pay for hurting others." When Taylor asks what Jordan means, Jordan replies, "You'll find out soon enough. You're cool, but other people need to watch their back." At first, Taylor thinks nothing of these statements as kids "blow off steam" all the time. Yet, Taylor also remembers their advisory group discussion that talked about noticing when someone is struggling and the importance of telling a trusted adult and getting help. Is this one of those times? Something doesn't feel right...

...

Targeted acts of violence at school are rare, but the impact is tremendous. While schools are supposed to be institutions focused on education, they are required to do so much more in regard to physical and psychological safety. The stress levels of our youth (and society in general) are at an all-time high. A recent study surveyed youth indicators of well-being. It showed that concerns about their present and future have increased, and upwards of 30 percent of young people say they have been feeling unhappy or depressed more often than not. They revealed more concern than usual about having their basic needs met. More than one-quarter of students (29 percent) reported not feeling connected at all to school adults, classmates, and/or their school community.[1]

In 2018, suicide was the second leading cause of death for individuals ages ten to twenty-four in the United States.[2] While there was a period of stability in the suicide rate from 2000 to 2007, the rate for this age group increased over 57 percent from 2007 to 2018![3] Current research is also showing the added effects of the COVID-19 pandemic. In a survey done during April–June of 2020, symptoms of anxiety disorder and depressive disorder increased considerably when compared with the same period in 2019.[4] And during a one-week period in June 2020, almost 11 percent of adults said they seriously considered suicide in the preceding thirty days.[5] The emotional stability of the caregiver/ parent, or lack thereof, can also directly impact a child's feeling of emotional and physical security.

While many think threats to schools would decrease with virtual instruction, that is not necessarily the case. The accumulation of stressors, many times coupled with feelings of discontent and physical and social isolation, can lead an individual to want to harm self and/or others as a way to cope. Schools, unfortunately, have been the target for acts of violence. Prior research conducted of active shooter incidences in the United States has shown that most perpetrators had significant difficulty coping with losses or failures, were feeling desperation or were despondent, and 78 percent of targeted mass attackers exhibited a history of suicide attempts or suicidal thoughts[6], with many attempting and 40 percent succeeding at suicide or "suicide by cop" at the conclusion of their targeted act of violence.[7] Thus homicidal and suicidal ideation can be closely linked.

In addition, while serious mental illness is often a substantial risk factor that is present in targeted acts of violence, it is important to note that it is not necessarily *the driving force* behind the decision to offend. *Most with a mental health diagnosis or illness will never be violent.* But serious mental health challenges are often co-occurring with other risk factor vulnerabilities (trauma history, substance abuse, environmental stressors, etc.), which can increase risk for harm to self and/or others and impact the ability to adaptively cope. In addition, research and analyses of completed acts of targeted school violence show that before a student committed an act of targeted violence on a school campus, warning signs were usually evident. Research also indicates that if appropriate action is taken when warning signs are recognized, the risk of violence can be mitigated.

This book will highlight the interrelated factors that play a role in a person's decision to plan and carry out an act of violence. Behavioral Threat Assessment and Management (BTAM) focuses on the behaviors of concern *and* also identifying resiliency and supports to help mitigate risk. Once these are understood, BTAM teams can work with the student, caregiver/parent, and educational team to manage behaviors, mitigate risk, and help the individual onto a more positive pathway. We know how to help someone who is suicidal or despondent. We can translate those skills into helping someone who is thinking of harming others.

In schools where threat assessment teams and protocols exist, educators and staff are more likely to engage in collaborative efforts to assess and appropriately manage (intervene with) a student who may pose danger to themselves or others. The goal of BTAM is to engage supports and help the student of concern onto a more positive pathway. *The goal is* not *punishment, as punishment alone does not change behaviors.* Rather, the timely response to a concern can enhance the safety of all students, including the individual of concern. The lives saved may include your own.

This book is intended to introduce school-based threat assessment to administrators, school mental health professionals, law enforcement/safety/security officers who serve schools, and other school and community-based professionals and support staff who are responsible for the safety and security of students and school communities. For those who already have a BTAM team and/or process in place, this book can help to refine and enhance already existing systems. For those who do not have a process in place, this book will provide good foundational knowledge to establish a quality BTAM process. In addition, the primary focus of this book is student(s) who make a threat and are the subject of concern. While chapter 3 briefly addresses workplace violence (when adults are the subject of concern) and many of the concepts in this book can be generalized to adults, additional knowledge is necessary to establish BTAM teams to assess adults of concern.

It also is important to note that reading this book does NOT replace receiving high quality training for team members by an expert who has worked actual K-12 cases. (See chapter 11 for training resources.) However, this book is a great resource to help establish, refine, and enhance your school/district's BTAM process.

Lastly, threats can still occur even if instruction is virtual. Additional guidance on how to conduct threat assessments in the virtual environment can be found in the downloadable resources.

What Is Behavioral Threat Assessment and Management (BTAM)?

Behavioral threat assessment and management (BTAM) is a fact-based, systematic process designed to identify, assess, and manage potentially dangerous or violent situations. BTAM focuses on "targeted acts of violence," which is defined as any "incident of violence where a known or knowable attacker selects a particular target prior to their violent attack."[8] The primary goal of school-based BTAM is to prevent the immediate risk of harm to others *and* engage resources and supports for the individual of concern. The United States Departments of Education, Justice, Secret Service, and Federal Bureau of Investigation, school safety experts, and law enforcement officials, have all cited research indicating that warning signs are usually evident before a student commits an act of violence on a school campus.[9,10] When threat assessment teams are established and well-trained, implement the process with fidelity, and act responsibly regarding the concern, students are more likely to receive counseling services and a parent conference, and they are less likely to receive long-term suspension or an alternative placement.[11]

There have been concerns that threat assessment leads to more students being placed into special education or the "school-to-prison" pipeline. This can occur when a threat assessment process is not used or when teams are not well trained. Research by Cornell and colleagues has shown that when implemented correctly, no disparities were found among Black, Hispanic, and White students in out-of-school suspensions, school transfers, or legal actions; thus a threat assessment process may reflect a generalizable pathway for achieving parity in school discipline.[12] While behavioral consequences (e.g., suspension) may need to be implemented in response to specific behaviors that violate policy or law, it must be paired with interventions and supports. BTAM helps prevent the overuse of suspension and expulsion and engages supports to guide an individual onto a more positive pathway.

U.S. Secret Service Model

The foundational content of this book is based on the Secret Service model for threat assessment. The Secret Service model is seen as the "gold standard," and is based on years of research to support the effectiveness of its implementation. It is used by many government entities and provides specific guidance for implementation in schools.

This model focuses on the following guiding principles[13]:

1. There is a distinction between *making* a threat and *posing* a threat.

2. Targeted violence is the end result of an understandable process of thinking and behavior.

2. Violence stems from interaction among subject, target, environment, and precipitating events (STEP).

4. Team members must have an investigative and inquisitive mindset.

5. Threat assessment is based upon facts and observations of behavior, not characteristics, traits, or profiles.

6. Threat assessment utilizes an integrated systems approach, with school-community partnerships utilized when needed.

While research has shown some commonalities between those who conduct targeted violent acts, there is no accurate profile of a "school shooter." Individuals don't "just snap." They engage in a process of escalating thoughts and behaviors. Therefore, multiple variables must be assessed and considered, and the interaction between the perpetrator, target, setting, and situation is considered. Team decisions are based upon objective data, not based upon profiling characteristics, stereotypes, personal biases, or misperceptions.

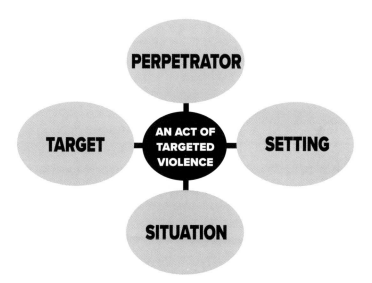

Eight-Step Process to Establishing a Quality BTAM Process

The National Threat Assessment Center (NTAC) and U.S. Secret Service and Department of Homeland Security (2018) outline eight critical steps to be included in a high-quality BTAM process.[14]

Step 1: Establish a Multidisciplinary Threat Assessment Team

Step 2: Define Prohibited and Concerning Behaviors

Step 3: Develop a Central Reporting Mechanism

Step 4: Determine the Threshold for Law Enforcement Intervention

Step 5: Establish Assessment Procedures

Step 6: Develop Risk Management Options

Step 7: Create and Promote Safe School Climates

Step 8: Conduct Training for All Stakeholders

Each of these steps will be addressed more in-depth in subsequent chapters. *Steps 7 and 8 are presented first in this book because they are critical to the foundation of a good BTAM process.*

Overview of BTAM Process

The BTAM process is designed to:

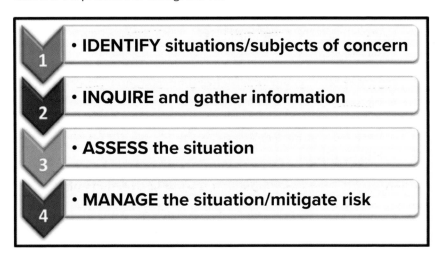

1
- **IDENTIFY situations/subjects of concern**

2
- **INQUIRE and gather information**

3
- **ASSESS the situation**

4
- **MANAGE the situation/mitigate risk**

Source: SIGMA Threat Management Associates (2017)

Clear and confidential reporting mechanisms must be in place to *identify* the subject/situation whose behavior or impact has raised concern. The multi-disciplinary BTAM school/district team then conducts an *inquiry* to gather additional information in a lawful and ethical manner. The situation is *assessed* to consider situational, contextual, developmental, and disability factors to determine if the subject/situation *poses* a threat of violence or harm to self and/or others. If there is a significant concern for safety, the BTAM team will engage law enforcement to determine if an official law enforcement investigation needs to begin. The situation is then *managed* by implementing problem-solving intervention and supports. If warranted, a formalized intervention, supervision, and monitoring plan is developed to engage supports, prevent harm, and reduce/mitigate impact of the situation.

In order to implement an effective process, specific **elements** of a quality BTAM process must be established. These include:

1. School/district establishing the authority and leadership to conduct the threat assessment inquiry

2. Developing a multi-disciplinary threat assessment team and providing high-quality, ongoing training

3. Establishing integrated and interagency systems relationships and partnerships

4. Providing awareness training for staff, students, parents, and community partners

Each of these elements will be discussed more in-depth in subsequent chapters.

It is important to note that BTAM is a deductive and dynamic process of reasoning to reach a logical conclusion with the focus on understanding and mitigating safety concerns. As more information comes forward, the team will need to interview more persons and collect additional data. It is *not* the same as a criminal or disciplinary investigative process, nor is it profiling. Profiling involves making generalizations about an individual based on the individual's similarity to high-risk groups, whereas threat assessment is an individualized assessment of the person of concern, considering their particular situation at a particular point in time.

Making a Threat vs. Posing a Threat

A key goal of BTAM is to distinguish between *making* a threat and *posing* a threat. One of most important distinctions, and most common mistakes, in school-based threat assessment is that all threats are treated as equal when they are not. An individual can make a threat and not pose a threat, and a person can pose a threat but may have never made an outward threat.

Making a threat is when someone says or does something that may concern others. Threats can be made out of frustration or anger, in a humorous or joking manner, or they may be serious and legitimate. Without context, words are words, and actions are actions; it is context that gives the threat meaning.

For example, have you ever looked at your spouse, significant other, or children and said, "If you don't knock it off, I'm going to kill you right now"? You technically made a threat! However, do you pose a threat? Not likely. The context needs to be assessed. For those who make a threat (but do not pose a threat), the situation can and should be handled through problem solving or existing supports, i.e., referral to student intervention team; counseling for anger management, depression, anxiety; mentoring; etc.

Posing a threat is when context, concerning variables, risk factors, and warning signs all support legitimacy to the threat, and the individual is exhibiting pathway behaviors. Interventions and supports must be engaged immediately to mitigate risk.

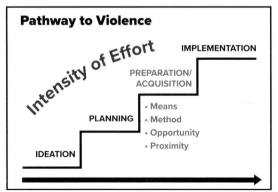

Pathway to Violence

Intensity of Effort

IMPLEMENTATION

PREPARATION/
ACQUISITION

PLANNING
- Means
- Method
- Opportunity
- Proximity

IDEATION

Source: SIGMA
Threat Management
Associates (2017)

Pathway behaviors characterize an individual who may *pose* a threat. Pathway behaviors begin with ideation. This is when an individual begins to have **ideation** (thinking) about wanting to harm others. If the pathway is not interrupted, the individual begins to **plan** their attack. In most previous K-12 school shooting attacks, the perpetrator did extensive research on prior school shootings, and this information better informed their plan.

If the planning is not interrupted, the individual then proceeds to **preparation/acquisition,** when they begin to gather the materials needed to execute the plan. They consider the means needed to execute their method (e.g., obtaining guns and ammunition, bomb-making materials), they research the most opportune time to carry out their plan (before school, during passing time, when the school resource officer/security officer or administrator is out of the building), and they research how to gain close proximity to their victims (i.e., which doors are unlocked, when the door monitor most often steps away from the door). If this preparation is not interrupted, the perpetrator then proceeds to **implementation** of the violent act.

On a positive note, at any point in time before implementation, the pathway can be interrupted and the individual provided interventions and supports to help them onto a more positive pathway. For individuals demonstrating pathway behaviors, it is often a cry for help because supports and coping resources have been insufficient or inaccessible to offset accumulating stressors. Once supports are engaged, many students have been successfully helped off the pathway to violence.

BIG Mistake Made in Schools

One of the biggest mistakes made in schools is when one person (rather than the team) makes the decision on how to handle a potential threat, and/or when teams do not follow the BTAM process. The report of a threat is received (identify) and a school professional(s) jumps to management (i.e., suspension or expulsion) rather than following the BTAM protocol. When time is not taken to properly inquire and assess, students can receive significant consequences (i.e., suspension, expulsion, placement in alternative school) for a statement or behavior that was not a true threat and/or due to personal biases or systemic discriminatory practices interfering with objective decision making. In schools, we work with a variety of diverse populations, developmental ages, developmental disabilities, and age groups whose frontal lobe is not fully developed; youth can act or speak impulsively without fully understanding the consequences. By not appropriately conducting all steps in the process, the course of students' educational careers can be significantly and negatively impacted by untrained professionals or professionals who are negligent in following best practices training. This can also erode trust within the school community. Students will stop reporting if every concern brought forward results in overly punitive consequences without a thorough BTAM assessment.

The flip side can also occur. If quick decisions are made based upon biases or personal opinions/feelings, a legitimate and "true" threat with pathway behaviors may be missed. For example, an administrator or teacher might say, "That student would never do that. They come from a nice family. They are our star athlete or scholar with so much going for them. They would never do anything to harm someone else." Remember, there is no single predictive profile of a perpetrator. School professionals and teams MUST follow the process. This helps prevent disproportionality in special education and discipline and helps avoid the school-to-prison pipeline. Failure to follow the process can also lead to claims of negligence or violation of due process (see Chapter Two).

Types of Threats

A threat is an expression of intent to cause harm. It can be communicated verbally, visually, in writing, electronically (i.e., social media), or through other means, and it has the potential to significantly disrupt the school or workplace environment.

Threats fall into four main categories:

TYPE OF THREAT	DEFINITION	EXAMPLE
Direct	Statement of clear, explicit intent to harm; plan is communicated; usually target is identified	"I am going to kill Mr. Smith for expelling me."
Indirect	Violence is implied or phrased tentatively	"I could do it if I wanted to." "You'll be sorry."
Conditional	Statement is made contingent on a set of circumstances	"*If* he's here tomorrow we'll get him back for what he did."
Veiled	Vague and subject to interpretation; oftentimes drawings, poetry, social media posts, and gestures fall into this category	"I just wish this entire place would go away." "I am sick and tired of everyone." "Does it ever get any better than this?"

It is important to note that context is more important than content, as most offenders do not directly threaten targets. Therefore, you cannot wait to receive a direct threat to begin the BTAM process.

Context is what also gives words and action meaning. Do these words concern you?

Nightmare	Blood	Devil	Knife
Skin	Kill	Cut	Destruction
Rip	Thrashing	Threatening	God

Now put them into context:

"The weather was a nightmare as the threatening tornado approached with intent to kill. My skin felt like it was going to rip right off as the winds came thrashing through town. It was

like the Devil took a knife and cut right though the center of town leaving destruction only on one side. I will never forget the sight of blood, but thank goodness God was watching over us and no one died."

Do these words below concern you?

Pretty	Flowers	Welcome	Beautiful
God	Place	Life	Meal

In isolation, probably not. Now put the words into context.

"You'd better get your life in order, buy pretty flowers, and enjoy your last meal because God has ordered me to take you to a beautiful place and he's more than ready to welcome you."

Does this now concern you? It should.

Without assessing context, risk factors, and warning signs, there is the risk of under- or over-responding, determining an inappropriate level of concern, and delivering inappropriate intervention and supports that could cause more harm. Many students have been suspended or expelled for *making* a threat when they did not *pose* a threat, and this can lead to many unintended consequences for their own future as well as the trust your school community has in the validity of the process. If data shows they pose a legitimate threat, management and supports are needed to ensure safety for all.

In summary, the BTAM process must be implemented with fidelity in order to increase chances of violent behavior being appropriately identified and risk mitigated. Violence is preventable, and the school/district threat assessment team is a critical component to school safety.

Case Study

There has been an increase in verbal aggression incidents over the past two months, both online and in person. Students are making comments such as, "I am going to take you out if you don't knock it off"; "I hate this school and everyone in it"; "Teachers are stupid and need to be eliminated." Online posts include pictures of graphic video game scenes, military soldiers holding weapons, and emojis conveying anger and frustration. This has led to multiple office referrals for discipline and numerous suspensions. The school counselor overheard a group of students talking about how you can "get permission to miss school" (i.e., get suspended) if you just say something that sounds threatening. While these statements need to be taken seriously, the school mental health team is concerned that the suspensions could be reinforcing negative behaviors. Referrals to the alternative education program have also significantly increased, and that program is frustrated they are "becoming a babysitting service." In addition, state legislation is likely to pass next month, mandating that threat assessment teams be established in schools. Something needs to change, but how?

1. How would you explain BTAM to the school leadership/administrative team?

2. How could the BTAM process help your school and prevent overuse of suspension and alternative placements?

3. What is the difference between making a threat and posing a threat?

4. Why is context so important when assessing risk?

KEY POINTS

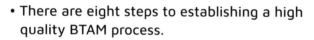

- There are eight steps to establishing a high quality BTAM process.
- The BTAM process is designed to identify, inquire, assess, and manage the situation.
- A key goal is to distinguish between making a threat and posing a threat.
- The pathway to violence includes ideation, planning, preparation/acquisition, and implementation.
- Threats can be direct, indirect, conditional, or veiled.
- BTAM principles and processes must be implemented thoroughly and with fidelity to avoid unintended consequences.

2 BTAM Legal and Ethical Considerations

Threat assessment is an important component to comprehensive school safety. Previous acts of violence have brought increased attention to targeted school violence, leading to many states passing laws requiring the establishment of BTAM teams and protocols.[15] In addition, multiple reports and government agencies have recommended schools establish threat assessment policies, procedures, and teams (e.g., US Departments of Homeland Security, Secret Service, Justice, and Education; Arapahoe High School post incident reports; Sandy Hook Advisory Commission; and Marjory Stoneman Douglas High School Public Safety Commission). As a result, schools are expected to have protocols in place to address targeted violence concerns. In addition, when threat assessment teams and protocols exist, educators, support staff, and law enforcement officials are more likely to work collaboratively to share information about students who may pose danger to themselves or others to effectively intervene.

It is important that school districts establish the authority to conduct a threat assessment and understand the limits to confidentiality and information sharing. District legal representation must also understand school safety laws and be consulted when developing BTAM policy and procedures.

Creating Policy

School boards should adopt a threat assessment policy that establishes authority for school professionals to act upon reported threats and/or concerning behaviors. While policies are specific to each district, it is recommended that a threat assessment policy include the following:

- Establishment of threat assessment teams at the school and/or district level

- Authority for responsibility of who shall establish these teams

- Roles and duties to be performed by designated BTAM members

- Expertise and training of professionals who will serve on the BTAM team

- Awareness training for staff, students, and parents

- Threat assessment protocol, procedures, and documentation, including exceptions to confidentiality

- Reporting procedures and requirements (i.e., mandatory reporters)

- Procedures for implementation of interventions, supports, and community services

- Timeframe required to responsibly act upon reported concern

- Engagement of school resource officers (SRO)/law enforcement to include parameters of information sharing

- Clearly defined guidelines for when searches can be conducted (e.g., locker, backpack, clothing, email/internet histories on school-issued electronic devices; vehicles, cell phones, etc.)

- Clearly defined authority to inquire/assess when concerning behaviors are reported, including behaviors that originate off school grounds or outside of school hours

- An expectation to consider alternatives to suspension and expulsion to facilitate a collaborative intervention approach

- Procedures for disciplinary actions and/or change of educational placement, if appropriate and warranted

Legal Guidelines for Information Sharing

One of the greatest impediments to information sharing is a concern regarding confidentiality. Many educators do not appropriately understand the limits to confidentiality, which means critical information is not shared when it can and should be.

* The information shared below is offered as general information, not formal legal advice.

Information Sharing and FERPA

FERPA (Family Educational Rights and Privacy Act) contains a "health or safety emergency exception" that allows school officials to disclose PII (personally identifiable information) from educational records without consent to appropriate parties when there is an actual, impending, or imminent emergency, such as an articulable and significant threat.[16] Schools have discretion to determine what constitutes a health and safety emergency and who are "appropriate parties." Typically, this includes school professionals with expertise in education, mental health, and behavioral interventions, law enforcement/school resource officers (SRO), first responders, public health officials (i.e., pandemic), and trained medical personnel. If a specific target is identified, and there is a legitimate impending or imminent threat, those intended targets must be notified. Authorities have a duty to inform and warn affected people/groups.

However, schools must balance safety with student privacy interests. Only school officials with a legitimate educational interest may access FERPA-protected education records, and schools are responsible for determining who is considered a "school official with a legitimate educational interest." Generally, this includes those professionals identified in the preceding paragraph. Non-school employees, whose professional expertise can help to address school safety concerns, may also be designated as school officials for the purpose of serving on a BTAM team if they meet certain criteria (i.e., SRO/law enforcement).

In addition, the information disclosed must be related to the specific presenting concern and disclosed only to protect the health and/or safety of students or other individuals. The FERPA exception is limited to the period of the emergency and does not allow for a blanket release of PII (personally identifiable information). The exception does not allow for disclosures for emergencies that *might* occur but does allow for disclosure when evidence substantiates a strong likelihood that violence will occur without disclosure, and the exception covers only educational records. It is recommended that MOUs (Memorandums of Understanding) are established between school districts and supporting agencies (i.e., law enforcement, community mental health agencies/providers) and that BTAM team members sign a written agreement stating they understand the FERPA limits and exceptions to sharing information.

FERPA does not cover personal knowledge or observations, so professionals may share their personal observations if asked about a significant safety concern. For example, if a teacher overhears a student making threatening remarks to another student, the teacher can share with appropriate parties. However, if a school official learns information about a student through their official role in creating or maintaining an educational record (e.g., suspension), then that information is covered by FERPA and must meet the FERPA exceptions to disclose.

Misinterpretations of FERPA exceptions have hindered prior efforts to conduct a thorough threat assessment, so it is important that schools understand and appropriately utilize the health or safety emergency exception. School officials should always consult with

full of risk factors (i.e., adverse childhood experiences) and little resiliency and supports, the outcome might be vastly different, with a disconnected student, added stress and trauma, and a lost opportunity to engage supports.

The lack of well-trained professionals and a fair and equitable team process to gather and analyze the data before making a decision can do more harm and send an individual down a more negative pathway, and there can also be unintended consequences. For example, Heather's senior year was miserable because she and her mom were blamed for getting Sarah kicked out of school, and Heather's peers never fully accepted her back into their social circles. Six months later, a student created a legitimate hit list but peers waited seven days to report because they did not trust the administrator(s) to handle it appropriately. They were concerned the student would be kicked out of school and would come back and "shoot up the school."

Students, staff, and parents must trust the BTAM process or they will not report. If consequences must be implemented, they must be reasonable for the level of concern and the student(s) and family must know that school professionals care.

QUESTIONS to CONSIDER
(Sarah)

1. How would your school(s) handle Sarah's situation?

2. What could the administrator have done differently?

3. How would your school(s) BTAM team ensure the BTAM process is not ignored in the future?

4. What other unintended consequences could arise if the incident between Sarah and Heather happened at your school(s)?

KEY POINTS

- School boards should establish a BTAM policy ensuring state laws are followed.

- FERPA (and HIPAA) exceptions to confidentiality must be clearly understood and utilized.

- A BTAM process for workplace violence should also be established.

- Best practices engage a multidisciplinary approach, with legal and ethical guidelines followed.

Foundations to Effective Threat Assessment and Management

Steps 7 and 8

Positive school climate and culture, relationships, connectedness, and a shared ownership for school safety are the best tools to prevent and mitigate targeted acts of school violence.

Create and Promote Safe School Climates (Step 7)

While listed as Step 7 in the BTAM Model, establishing a safe school climate should be prioritized as Step 1. Threat assessment is most effective and successful when embedded within a comprehensive multi-tiered system of supports. Efforts to improve school climate, safety, and learning are not and should not be separate endeavors. Interdisciplinary collaborative partnerships focused on prevention and early intervention prevent stressors from escalating.

Multi-Tiered System of Supports (MTSS)

A Framework for Safe and Successful Schools specifies best practices for establishing safe and successful schools utilizing an interdisciplinary MTSS approach.[17] This framework helps to identify and engage students in need of additional supports before they enter onto the pathway to violence. Practices include the following:

- Universal screening for academic, behavioral, and emotional barriers to learning

- Implementing a high-quality, rigorous, developmentally appropriate curriculum that addresses core academic competencies, social-emotional learning (SEL) principles, mental and behavioral wellness, *and* positive behaviors (i.e., positive behavior supports)

- Regular review of student behavioral and academic data to guide early identification and progress monitoring of interventions

- Engaging multidisciplinary, data-based decision-making team(s) made up of principals/administrators, teachers (general and special education), parents, school-employed mental health professionals (e.g., school psychologists, counselors, social workers), and other specialized instructional support personnel

- Access to high-quality, early-intervention, evidence-based academic and social-emotional interventions to address the comprehensive needs of students

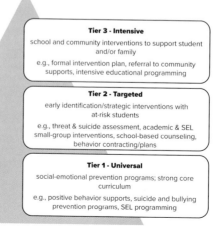

Tier 3 - Intensive
school and community interventions to support student and/or family
e.g., formal intervention plan, referral to community supports, intensive educational programming

Tier 2 - Targeted
early identification/strategic interventions with at-risk students
e.g., threat & suicide assessment, academic & SEL small-group interventions, school-based counseling, behavior contracting/plans

Tier 1 - Universal
social-emotional prevention programs; strong core curriculum
e.g., positive behavior supports, suicide and bullying prevention programs, SEL programming

SEL Curriculum

While a strong academic curriculum is certainly important, given the multitude of stressors our students have experienced (i.e., pandemic; social, political, and civil unrest; increasing mental health concerns), the integration of a universal social-emotional learning (SEL) curriculum is critical.

The Collaborative for Academic, Social, and Emotional Learning (CASEL) is a leader in SEL implementation and programming. CASEL's five core competency areas include:

Properly implemented SEL curricula have shown the following outcomes[18]:

- improvement in students' social and emotional skills, attitudes, relationships, and academic performance

- improved classroom behavior

- increased ability to manage stress and depression, better attitudes and perceptions about themselves, others, and school

- decline in students' anxiety, behavior problems, and substance use

- statistically significant associations between SEL skills in kindergarten and key outcomes for young adults years later

SEL lessons include the following topics that help to promote and sustain a safe school climate: diversity and inclusion, emotional regulation, conflict resolution, problem-solving skills, bullying, suicide, and violence prevention. In addition, diversity is celebrated and accepted. While there has been much focus on the word "tolerance," people don't want to be tolerated; they want to be accepted.

Positive Behavior Supports

Positive behavior supports (PBS) is a framework that focuses on establishing positive behaviors in schools. At the universal level (Tier 1), school-wide prosocial skills and behavioral expectations are established. Students are engaged in establishing these expectations and positive behaviors are rewarded. At Tier 2, there is early engagement with students at risk and social-emotional interventions are provided (i.e., social skills, emotional regulation skills, academic supports). At Tier 3, intervention and supports are more individualized and community wraparound services may be engaged.

SEL and PBS complement each other, with a focus on building a positive school climate and culture. Analysis of a school's academic, behavioral, and social-emotional data can guide data-based decisions regarding the specific areas where prevention and intervention programs could be most helpful. See chapter 11 for additional SEL resources.

Conduct Training for All Stakeholders (Step 8)

Training Students, Staff, and Community

BTAM team decisions are only as good as the information coming forward, so universal prevention programming must include direct and comprehensive training for all stakeholders (students, teachers, support staff, coaches, mentors, parents, community members) so they know how and when to report concerns (see chapter 5). This training cannot be a one-time event that happens only at the beginning of the school year. It must be embedded within universal SEL/PBS programming. This training must include the difference between tattling (telling an adult to get someone in trouble) versus telling (telling an adult to help someone who is struggling or when others are in danger). In addition, the saying that "snitches get stiches" must be addressed directly so students are willing to break the code of silence to engage help and also encourage others to report concerns. This same message also needs to be reinforced to the community so concerns are reported.

Training BTAM Teams

It is critical for BTAM teams to receive proper training by qualified professionals who have experience working in schools, have served on threat assessment teams, *and* have worked K-12 threat assessment cases. School administrators need to vet the credentials of trainers carefully. Many companies offer training services, but not all have the proper credentials or experience in working K-12 cases. In some cases, companies push an online product in order to store and analyze your threat assessments records in the absence of on-site training. BTAM teams must know *how* to conduct the process and analyze the data to reach validated and appropriate conclusions.

BTAM training should encompass the eight steps that serve as the framework for this book and should not include the "sharing of war stories." Showing graphic videos and images is not only disrespectful to victims and survivors, but it is also unnecessary and can traumatize participants. Good BTAM trainers:

- Minimize trauma exposure

- Have an in-depth understanding of the K-12 environment, including a solid understanding of child and adolescent development and working with students with special needs

- Are knowledge regarding K-12 instructional service delivery models

- Understand child and adolescent mental and behavioral health

- Provide knowledge of FERPA privacy laws and limitations to confidentiality

- Train how to facilitate effective collaboration and communication within a large system that addresses diverse needs

Pick and vet your professional development opportunities and trainers carefully!

To summarize steps 7 and 8, the BTAM process supports comprehensive school safety and facilitates increased academic and school engagement. The BTAM process interfaces with other processes and supports that are already established in schools. Collaborative partnerships between schools, community agencies, and providers, parents, and students help ensure successful BTAM outcomes.

Case Study

The stressors of the past year have been difficult for everyone. While in-person instruction has resumed, everyone seems to be in a "fog." The excitement that used to radiate the halls has been tempered, students and staff are stressed, and academic engagement is lower than pre-pandemic levels. Referrals for suicidal ideation have also increased, and there are not enough school mental health professionals to meet the individual needs. School-wide initiatives focused on increasing social-emotional supports are needed.

QUESTIONS to CONSIDER

Which of the following does your school have in place to facilitate a positive school climate and a solid BTAM foundation?

✓ Positive behavior supports/MTSS	✓ Confidential reporting system
✓ Peer mentors	✓ De-escalation training for staff
✓ Adult mentors	✓ Trauma-informed/sensitive training for staff
✓ Student leadership activities	✓ Data-driven decision-making processes and teams
✓ Prevention programs that celebrate diversity, inclusiveness, and acceptance	✓ Buddy classes (older students will mentor/engage in activities with younger students; "reading buddies")
✓ SEL and mental health programming (e.g., bullying prevention, suicide prevention)	✓ Opportunities for staff and students to engage in non-academic activities (e.g., field day, talent show, classroom buddies)
✓ Universal academic and social-emotional screenings	✓ Monitoring of reactions to grievances and engagement of supports
✓ Rigorous yet developmentally appropriate academic curriculum	✓ Established system for students to seek support proactively from an adult

KEY POINTS

- A positive school climate is the foundation for any good BTAM process.
- High quality training is critical. Trainers must have direct experience working actual K-12 threat assessment cases and a solid understanding of the K-12 educational environment.
- Prevention and collaborative relationships are key!

Establish the Multi-Disciplinary Team

Step 1

Prior to conducting threat assessments, a multi-disciplinary BTAM team must be selected carefully and receive appropriate training. The size and resources of the school/district will impact which structure is best. The graphic below demonstrates the three main team structures that support a BTAM process.

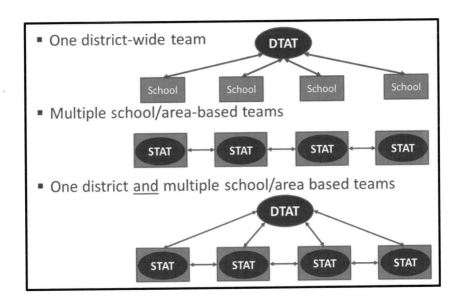

- One district-wide team
- Multiple school/area-based teams
- One district <u>and</u> multiple school/area based teams

One District-Wide Team

In this model, a district-level team handles all threat assessment cases regardless of the school or age of the potential perpetrator. The district team triages the referral, and if a full BTAM assessment is needed, the district team leads the full threat assessment with input and data gathered from the school-level professionals who know the student(s)/situation. A district-level team is more commonly used in smaller school districts and/or in rural areas with itinerant professionals (school professionals assigned multiple schools who may only be at a particular school on select days of the week) or when resources at the individual school level are limited.

Multiple School/Area-Based Teams

In this model, each school has its own BTAM team. There is no district-level team for support, so if additional supports and/or guidance is needed, the school team needs to ensure collaborative partnerships have been established with community resources (i.e., community-based BTAM team) or other area school teams. This model is often used in independent and private schools.

One-District Team and Multiple School Teams

In this model, a central district-level team(s) provides consultation, oversight, consistency, and accountability for all BTAM processes at the school level. The district-level team also helps to manage threats impacting more than one school in the district. BTAM teams are also established at each school to receive the referral and proceed with the full threat assessment, if needed. In more serious cases, the school team can engage the district team for additional consultation and support. This model is the ideal, particularly for districts/regions with multiple schools. While most cases can be managed at the school level, this model provides extra support. It also ensures that school teams have the resources and training needed to ensure a high-quality BTAM process is implemented.

BTAM Team Membership

The multi-disciplinary BTAM team must be carefully selected *and* receive appropriate BTAM training because most professional training programs have not included school-based threat assessment in their preservice training. Involving an array of disciplines enhances the team's ability to:

- Identify developing concerns/threats

- Gather information from multiple sources

- Decrease organizational "silos" and increase cross-collaboration and communication within the school and with community support providers

- Maximize skills and resources to address concerns

- Monitor outcomes

- Collaborate regarding effective awareness and outcomes

- Coordinate and engage in purposeful actions and interventions to mitigate risk and engage the individual(s) of concern onto a more positive pathway

The BTAM team should include representation from the following areas of expertise:

- school administration
- counseling/mental health
- behavior management
- classroom instruction
- special education
- school resource officer/law enforcement
- school safety/security/emergency management

With limited resources, some schools/districts may not have the resources for one specific person to represent each of these areas, so one professional could represent multiple areas of expertise. For example, school psychologists have expertise in counseling/mental health, behavior management, instructional interventions, identifying learning and developmental disabilities, and special education. Including a school psychologist on the team allows for multiple areas of expertise to be represented. With that said, the team cannot be too small, because diversity in thought and perspectives is needed. Back-up team members also need to be identified and appropriately trained.

Core Team

The core team should have representation that *at minimum* includes at least one administrator, *at least* one, preferably two, school mental health professionals (school psychologist, school counselor, school social worker, school nurse), and a school resource officer (SRO)/law enforcement official (LEO). The core team is responsible for conducting the screening (see chapter 6) and leading the full threat assessment, if needed. If a full assessment is conducted, the core team is responsible for the process and the decisions made by the BTAM team, with input provided by additional team members (see below).

Case Manager/Team Leader

From the core team, it is highly recommended a case manager/team leader is selected. The case manager/team leader does not do all the work, but they are to ensure the process is conducted thoroughly, ethically, legally, and with fidelity. The case manager is also responsible for ensuring proper documentation is completed and retained according to district guidelines and federal and state laws.

School Administrator

The school administrator is typically responsible for ensuring the team members are trained and execute their duties. In addition, the administrator(s):

- Consults with core team members to screen cases and determine if full threat assessment inquiry needs to be conducted

- Assists in interviewing subjects, targets, witnesses, teachers, staff, parents, and students

- Assists in gathering information

- Enforces disciplinary consequences, if appropriate

- Ensures the threat management plan is followed and monitored

- Ensures intervention and supports are being provided

- Works closely with the public information officer or communications director to respond to community concerns and questions

- Facilitates a collaborative process focused on interventions and supports

See chapter 8 for additional school administrator leadership, management, and collaboration responsibilities.

School Mental Health Professional (School Psychologist/Social Worker/Counselor/Nurse)

The school's mental health professionals often take the lead in the initial conversations and interviews because they are trained in how to conduct interviews without asking leading questions. In addition, since their roles are non-disciplinary and they are perceived as more "neutral," students are typically more forthcoming with information.

Mental health professionals also understand child and adolescent development and the interaction of social, cognitive, and moral development. This understanding is critical when conducting a threat assessment, because risk for violence can change depending on how an individual perceives the issues, stressors, and experiences and their developmental relevance for that individual. For example, adolescents are more heavily influenced by peer pressure, social media, social identity, and peer acceptance. So, psychological injury resulting from peer victimization or other cumulative stressors can move an adolescent to exhibit more extreme behaviors to exact revenge, to improve their social standing, or to "settle a score" to maintain their social standing. Students also say or do things without fully understanding the consequences. They have less developed reasoning ability and impulse control.

While communicated threats of violence should never be ignored, the school mental health professionals' understanding of typical and atypical development helps in the accurate differentiation between making a threat and posing a threat. This increases accuracy of the BTAM assessment and improves the team's ability to manage risk and take actions that match the level of concern. This accuracy also helps minimize the risk of further contributing to disproportionality in disciplinary practices and/or special education programming decisions.

In addition, school mental health professionals:

- Consult with administration and other core team members to screen cases to determine if a full threat assessment inquiry is needed

- Lead and/or assist in conducting interviews of subjects, targets, witnesses, teachers, staff, parents, and students

- Assist in gathering information

- Serve as a liaison with community mental health providers

- Advise the team on school-based and community

interventions and supports, including possible mental health assessments, where appropriate

- Provide interventions and supports

- Assists with next steps and possible referrals

- Facilitate progress monitoring

- Conduct a suicide risk assessment if suicidal indictors are present

School Resource Officer (SRO)/Law Enforcement Officer (LEO)

SRO/LEOs are critical members to any threat assessment team, and in many states the SRO/LEO role must be represented on the team. While there have been recent concerns about law enforcement presence in schools, a properly trained SRO is a valuable asset to a BTAM team because they often have critical information regarding school and community dynamics. Their involvement on BTAM teams can be consultative in nature, or it can be more directive if there is a serious and imminent threat. See chapter 2 and downloadable resources for more information regarding SRO/LEO's access to FERPA protected educational records when serving on a BTAM team.

Specific SRO/LEO duties many include:

- Assisting with gathering information

- If appropriate, assisting in conducting interviews of subjects, targets, witnesses, teachers, staff, parents, and students*

- Assisting with efforts to ensure safety and security

- Serving as a liaison with law enforcement, court personnel, juvenile justice, probation, etc.

- Determining the need for welfare checks, weapons checks, and home searches, where permissible

- Assisting with next steps and possible referrals

- Providing intervention supports, monitoring, and engagement

- Conducting independent criminal investigations, as needed

See chapter 8 for additional SRO/LEO responsibilities in management and collaboration.

* When involved in conducting interviews, is the SRO/LEO acting as a school official or as a law enforcement agent? This has been tested in court filings. School officials have more flexibility in questioning in regard to safety concerns. If acting as a law enforcement agent and/or it is perceived the questioning was investigative in nature, lawyers have argued Miranda Rights needed to be read and other procedures for "interrogating" minors needed to be followed. This is beyond the scope of this book, but it needs to be clearly understood and addressed in the MOU (memorandum of understanding) between school districts and law enforcement agencies, and when schools/districts are identifying "school officials" within their district policies and procedures.

Additional Team Members

In addition to core team members, other professionals with knowledge of the person of concern and/or situation must be engaged in the process. They could be asked to join the threat assessment team, or at minimum, they can provide perspectives on the dynamics surrounding the concern, ideas for potential intervention and management, and knowledge of additional sources of information. Considering various perspectives and input is valuable to the BTAM team's decision.

Additional ad hoc team members may include:

- general education teachers
- special education teachers
- special education case manager
- safety/security specialist

- behavior specialist
- coaches/advisors
- school mentors
- mental health therapist (if providing services in the school setting)

Other professionals may also have important information to contribute on a case-by-case basis, but typically do not serve on the BTAM team. These include:

- teaching assistants
- bus drivers
- secretaries
- school support staff (e.g., reading specialist)
- before and after school director/staff
- community-based resource professionals (e.g., social services)

If the situation warrants, the involvement of district legal counsel may be necessary. It is important that they stay abreast of school safety laws and precedent-setting legal cases since school safety law is a relatively new territory for educational lawyers.

If an employee is involved (employee made a threat or is on the receiving end of the threat), a representative from human resources may also need to be engaged.

External Consultants

In situations where additional expertise and/or experience is needed, the school team may choose to engage an outside threat assessment expert, someone not employed by the school/district. It is critical that this expert has specific expertise in working K-12 threat assessment cases and understands the school setting and educational service delivery requirements. Examples include:

- **Threat Management Specialist**
  - Has relevant education, training, and experience to assist with challenging cases
  - Provides consultation and coaching regarding consistency and implementation of process
  - Provides professional development to BTAM teams

- **Independent medical/psychological evaluator**
  - Has specific professional expertise in conducting clinical violence risk assessments/forensic evaluations
  - Understands the needs and resources of your school/district and is willing to work *with* school/district BTAM teams regarding recommended interventions
  - Willing to share information with BTAM teams with appropriate consent

For serious or complex cases, the BTAM team may determine a clinical assessment is needed. Schools/districts need to have a pre-established relationship with at least one (and preferably two to three) highly qualified evaluators. This allows parents to select from a provided list of qualified professionals. Schools/districts also need to understand the costs and processes for recommending or mandating an outside assessment. If recommended or mandated by a school/district, the school/district may have to pay the cost. There are also legal implications (and possibly accusations of denying educational services) if a student is not allowed to return to school until an outside evaluation is conducted. Be sure the legalities are clear if engaging an outside evaluator.

It is also important to note that engaging an outside threat management specialist or evaluator *does not* absolve the school/district team from completing a thorough BTAM process, nor should it ever replace the school/district's BTAM process. This can actually increase potential negligence claims because schools are responsible for safety and providing educational services. In addition, if you are in a state that requires this process, the BTAM team can violate state law by not conducting a school-based BTAM assessment.

In addition, the school BTAM team has critical data and knowledge of situational and relationship dynamics that can impact risk determination. The person of concern may not share or can minimize critical information when the evaluation is being done by an outside expert. That expert also does not have access to the various individuals in a school setting to gather and validate critical information. Therefore, the school/district BTAM team should work collaboratively *with* any outside expert, and the report/input provided by an outside expert is considered alongside all other data the school/district team has gathered. As in any threat assessment case, timeliness is of concern, and the engagement of any resources and expertise should be done in an expeditious manner to avoid the potential escalation of the situation.

Team Collaboration

While professional expertise is important, BTAM team members must also possess specific personality traits that facilitate collaboration under stressful and time-sensitive circumstances. These include: being empathetic, intuitive, and a good listener; detail-oriented; the ability to build rapport and multi-task; and self-awareness and willingness to acknowledge own biases.

Team members must also understand and value the importance of:

- Caretaking and interventions to support individuals
- The need for urgency when responding to a concern
- Respectful collaboration, even when disagreeing
- Respecting BTAM rules and boundaries or limits of confidentiality
- Providing guidance and follow-through with intervention and support plans
- Continually re-evaluating active cases and re-engaging when necessary
- Patience

Awareness of Biases

An effective team encourages and supports self-awareness to minimize bias and to ensure all members maintain objectivity. If biases interfere, critical information can be missed or misinterpreted, thus leading to poor BTAM decisions. Described below are the most common biases that impact the BTAM process:

Implicit Bias	Attitudes or stereotypes that affect our understanding, actions, and decisions in an unconscious manner; feelings and attitudes about other people based on characteristics (e.g., race, ethnicity, age, appearance); associations (positive or negative) can develop at an early age; influenced by exposure to direct and indirect messages, including media and news
	e.g., Because Nijah is black, she is capable of more violence. Just watch the news, you see it all the time.
Explicit Bias	Attitudes and beliefs toward certain types of individual(s) or group on a conscious level; often a direct result of a perceived threat, thus more likely to draw group boundaries to distinguish themselves from others; racism and prejudices
	e.g., Because Johnny hangs around the "emo/goth" group, he is more likely to plan a violent attack.
Confirmation Bias	Tendency to look for evidence or interpret information in a way that confirms a preconceived opinion; notice facts that support own beliefs and ignore those that do not
	e.g., Mia is a high achieving, well-liked student from a good family. She would never harm anyone.
Availability Bias	Assign importance to behaviors that immediately come to mind; miss or overlook importance of older information; if current news story (e.g., recent school shooting), all referred threats are seen as serious—can lead to overuse and misuse of suspension and expulsion
	e.g., I've been working with Sarah and she's had three months of no office referrals for explosive behaviors. She's on a better path so I don't think this threat is legit.
Hindsight Bias	Occurs after an event; person(s) may see the event as more predictable than it really was; leads to blame or belief could have predicted or prevented
	e.g., Now that I look back at the situation, his anger was getting worse and there were more conflicts with peers. I thought the gun he was talking about was in a video game. I should have said something.

Groupthink Bias	More likely to align own opinions with the group majority; fear of dissenting
	e.g., The BTAM team concludes the student poses a low risk and you feel the student poses a moderate to high risk. You say to yourself, "Maybe I am overreacting," and you go along with the team's decision to not put formal supports in place. In a week the situation escalates to a serious, imminent threat.

We all have biases. Recognizing these biases in the BTAM process is critical to ensure fair and equitable decisions. Team members should feel comfortable to discuss openly how they are impacting individual perspectives and the team decisions.

In regard to hindsight bias, thorough documentation is critical. There should be a disclaimer on the paperwork that reflects the decision of the BTAM team was based upon information currently available and legally accessible at this moment in time.

Additional Group Pitfalls

When individuals say or do things that require multiple threat assessments (our "frequent fliers"), it is easy to become *desensitized* and to begin cutting corners with the assessment process. Teams cannot do this because each assessment is a different moment in time, and stressors and/or grievances may have changed. Each assessment needs to be treated as new and done thoroughly. The historical information already gathered can be utilized again, but the current situational factors need to be thoroughly reassessed.

Teams often conduct multiple interviews to gather information. Illusions of memory, inattentional blindness, and change blindness can impact how individuals perceive, remember, and report specific events they are being asked about.

Illusions of memory	When an individual's recollection of a past event is inconsistent with the actual occurrence
Change blindness	When a person fails to recognize an obvious change
Inattentional blindness	When individuals miss even the most conspicuous events unless they pay close attention

Illusions of memory can lead to misinformation or inconsistent information being conveyed to the BTAM team. An example of *change blindness* is failing to notice that an individual took off a red jacket and put on a black jacket, so law enforcement is still looking for the red jacket to identify the person of concern. How many times do you look at a sign while driving to work, but you cannot recollect what it says when asked? This is an example of *inattentional blindness* which can lead to missing key, obvious details.

Thus, teams always be sure to "triangulate the data" (multi-method, multi-source) and never rely on just one account. This is also why it is helpful to see the original writings, drawings, social media posts, etc. as these provide context and also help to minimize recollection errors or misperceptions.

Case Study

Remember the student in chapter 2 who had the legitimate hit list? His father took him to his psychologist who provided the father a one-page letter for the school. The letter contained one sentence that said, "He is safe to return to school." That psychologist never contacted any school professionals even though the school professionals had a list of risk factors, warning signs, and critical information this psychologist needed before determining risk. This evaluation was not worth the paper it was written on. Thank goodness the BTAM team followed its own BTAM process to engage additional supports and monitoring to prevent an act of violence from occurring.

In another serious case with complex mental health issues involved, the school district agreed to pay for the outside evaluation (by a vetted evaluator approved by the school district) to gather additional information to compliment the school's BTAM team assessment. The district superintendent readily agreed to pay the $2,500 and stated that there was no price tag that could be placed on safety. The students' parents agreed to sign the release of information, under the condition that the district paid. The information provided was invaluable to the BTAM team and the student's parents. This collaborative process helped to facilitate the engagement of additional intensive community and school mental health, educational, and family interventions, which successfully helped this student off the pathway to violence.

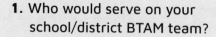

QUESTIONS to CONSIDER

1. Who would serve on your school/district BTAM team?

2. What training does your school/district team need?

3. What biases could come into play as your school/district works BTAM cases?

4. How would your team address differences of opinion?

KEY POINTS

- Establish a well-trained multi-disciplinary BTAM team. School administrators, school mental health professionals, and SRO/LEOs comprise the core team, with input received from others knowledgeable of concern.

- Team decisions must be based on objective facts, not emotions or biases. This helps mitigate disproportionality that exists within disciplinary practices.

- Self-awareness and team awareness of how biases may be impacting team decisions must be discussed openly.

- Back-up members and new BTAM members must be trained.

- Everyone must know their roles and be invested in prevention, intervention, and supports.

Identification and Reporting of Concerns

Define Concerning and Prohibited Behaviors (Step 2)

Develop a Central Reporting Mechanism (Step 3)

Determine Threshold for Law Enforcement Intervention (Step 4)

Responsible and accurate conclusions rely heavily on the information for which those decisions are based. It is important to identify which concerns are to be reported, explicitly teach how to report the concerns, and ensure those concerns reach the BTAM team.

Defining Concerning and Prohibited Behaviors

Schools have many different types of student intervention teams, so which concerns are reported to student intervention team(s) and which ones go to the BTAM team? This must be clearly defined, and intervention and BTAM teams must also not hesitate to refer concerns to each other. Schools serve a diverse population that includes a variety of developmental ages, disabilities, and emotional maturity levels. The frontal lobe (part of the brain that controls cognitive skills, emotional expression, problem solving, memory, language, judgment, and impulses) is not fully developed until at least mid-twenties. Due to their impulsivity and brain development, students may make a threat or sarcastic joke in response to a specific frustrating situation, but there is no genuine intent to harm. They do not pose a threat. Previous research suggests that as many as 70 percent of threats may be transient (do not pose a legitimate threat).[19]

However, some individuals may pose a threat, and the school community needs to be educated on behaviors that are unacceptable. Concerns that must be reported to the BTAM team include:

- engaging in violence
- threatening actions
- bringing a weapon to school
- significant bullying or harassing behavior
- risk factors (see chapter 6), paired with escalating behaviors or unexplained behavioral changes (change in demeanor, engagement)
- threats and/or communications that have context and meaning to support a legitimate safety concern
- person(s) on receiving end is concerned for their safety

The BTAM team may then choose to conduct a full threat assessment and/or engage other intervention team processes (i.e., Title IX, academic intervention, or behavior support team). It is better to over-report than to under-report because this allows the BTAM team to engage early, before more troublesome behaviors occur.

Note: Any mention of sexual harassment, sexual assault, stalking, domestic violence, or dating violence requires a report also be made to the Title IX Coordinator.

Threat to Comfort vs. Threat to Safety

Due to recent events and stressors, there has been an increase in volatility and a decrease in tolerance for differing viewpoints. These recent dynamics have led to increased reporting due to negative or differing viewpoints being expressed, which necessitates differentiating a threat to comfort and a threat to safety. A threat to comfort is when you feel uncomfortable because words or viewpoints expressed differ from your own, actions offend you because of your viewpoints, and/or personal implicit or explicit biases impacts your interpretation of the actual situation. A threat to safety is when you feel scared because actions and/or threats potentially put you or someone else in harm's way. When training on appropriate reporting, it is important to teach others about this distinction. While all reports must be taken seriously, the process must be followed to ensure a threat to comfort is not misidentified as a threat to safety, thus resulting in unfair or overly punitive measures.

Develop a Central Reporting Mechanism

The school community must know how to report potential threat, and there should be multiple ways to report: telling a trusted adult, email, phone call, text line, hotline, a reporting link on the school/district website, reporting app, and calling 911 for an imminent safety concern. It is important to have more than one confidential reporting method with explicit training on how to report a problem. Students must also be taught what is not appropriate to report (e.g., tattling vs. telling). Without this distinction, schools that have established electronic reporting mechanisms (i.e., reporting app, tip lines) have been overrun with inappropriate reports (i.e., "Johnny took my seat on the bus before I got on."). Regardless of which methods are available, every reporting method must be constantly monitored, and all pertinent information needs to be funneled to the BTAM team.

Considerable research has highlighted the effectiveness of established tip lines (i.e., Colorado's Safe 2 Tell[20]) when implemented after careful thought and with sufficient resources and infrastructure to support. School districts (and some states) have rushed into adopting a reporting app/tip line without thinking through the legal and financial implications. See Appendix A for a list of specific questions that must be considered before adopting any reporting app/tip line. Without addressing these considerations, staff can become easily overwhelmed, and the school/district can unknowingly increase their liability.

Overcoming the "Bystander Effect"

School communities must address the bystander effect, defined as noticing a concern but not reporting it. A positive school climate (chapter 3, step 7) will reinforce the message that when you report a possible threat, you are getting someone help, not getting someone in trouble.

When concerns are noticed, it is critical for reports to be taken seriously and handled responsibly (i.e., source remains confidential, actions taken are appropriate to the level of concern). If overly punitive actions are taken, students will stop reporting. They do not want to be responsible for getting a peer suspended or expelled from school. And, they don't want a peer to receive a serious punitive consequence only to find out the threat was not legitimate.

Cultural implications can also impact reporting. Communities with past traumas or incidents may not trust disclosing serious incidents to those in authority (i.e., "snitches get stitches"). When conducting awareness training, this lack of trust needs to be addressed through relationship building and through dialogue that addresses these concerns.

Determining the Threshold for Law Enforcement Intervention

Law enforcement is a critical member of any BTAM team. They often have knowledge regarding community dynamics in which the person of concern may be involved. In addition, they have insight regarding juvenile justice system involvement and other situational factors not readily known to school personnel. Their level of engagement is on a continuum; it can be more consultative or more directive. For lower-level concerns, they may consult and collaborate with the BTAM team on ideas for positive community engagement, relationship building, and decreasing individual, family, peer, and/or community stressors. If an imminent risk situation occurs (i.e., threats of violence, violent acts, weapon on campus, significant bullying behavior at the level of a criminal violation), then law enforcement would directly engage to assure the safety of the school community. While there are concerns about the "school-to-prison pipeline," appropriate law enforcement engagement in the BTAM process actually *prevents* the overuse of legal, punitive measures as a BTAM management tool. Many SROs have reported that when they are called to respond to a potential threat, school administration (or pressure from parents) expects them to arrest the student. They just want that student removed from the school, erroneously thinking the problem will be gone. This is not an appropriate use of SRO/LEOs. Administration needs to be trained on the appropriate use of SROs (see chapter 8).

It is important to emphasize that engagement of law enforcement does not relieve the BTAM team from conducting the school BTAM process. BTAM teams must continue to be engaged with the process for accurate assessment and successful management of the concern.

If the law enforcement officer is not a district staff employee, a memorandum of understanding (MOU) should be developed to outline the relationship between school staff and law enforcement, as well as law enforcement responsibilities in the BTAM process.

Privacy issues and access to educational records related to FERPA must also be addressed.[21] Additional information and sample MOUs can be found in the downloadable resources.

Case Study (Jordan)

Taylor was scared to say anything to get Jordan in trouble but was also scared that Jordan might harm others. Jordan's social media posts were escalating with themes of anger and discontent for those whom Jordan perceived as disrespecting unity and diversity. Even though school had just resumed in-person instruction, Jordan seemed more despondent than before. Taylor remembered what the school counselor said in the advisory meeting: "You are not narking, you are getting someone help. That's what we do at this school. We help each other, especially during these hard times." Taylor approached Mr. Lewis, the English teacher, and showed him the social media posts, along with concerns about changes in Jordan's behavior and emotions. The English teacher was also concerned and confirmed that Taylor had done the right thing by coming to him. Together, they reported these concerns to the BTAM team leader.

QUESTIONS to CONSIDER

1. Which behaviors would be reported to your school's student intervention team? Which ones would be reported to the BTAM team?

2. What reporting mechanisms are available in your school/district? How well are they monitored?

3. When would law enforcement intervene in your school(s)? What back-up plan is in place if law enforcement is unavailable?

KEY POINTS

- Differentiate and define which concerning behaviors are referred to student intervention teams and which prohibited behaviors are to be referred to the BTAM team.

- Identify the central reporting mechanisms and provide direct instruction on how and when to use them.

- To "break the code of silence" and overcome the bystander effect, students must trust the BTAM process will be handled responsibly and discretely.

- Law enforcement engagement can be consultative or directive depending on presenting concern.

Establish BTAM Assessment Procedures

Step 5

Thorough implementation of BTAM principles and assessment procedures must be in place to ensure a fair and equitable process. As stated previously, it is important to establish confidential and accessible reporting mechanisms to identify the subject(s)/situation(s) of concern. The BTAM team must then conduct a screening to determine if a full threat assessment needs to be conducted in a lawful and ethical manner. Personal, situational, contextual, developmental, and disability factors all must be considered to determine if the subject poses a threat of violence or harm to self and/or others. This chapter will discuss how teams should identify, inquire, assess, and manage threats by utilizing screening, data collection, and guidelines for analysis of data, which then drives the management (intervention) decisions.

Recent research from the Secret Service[22] shows there is still no accurate or useful profile of a "school shooter," nor is there one specific reason that increases risk. While grievances were often evident in the K-12 cases of violence, multiple motives and stressors were also significant contributing factors. The most common factor was grievance was between the perpetrator and a classmate, followed by grievances with school staff, a romantic relationship, or personal issues. Most perpetrators experienced psychological, behavioral, or developmental symptoms. One of the most critical findings was that ALL offenders exhibited concerning behaviors, with most communicating their intent to others. Thus, interviewing those with pertinent information, good data collection, and awareness training that addresses "breaking the code of silence" are all critical elements to preventing acts of violence. Pertinent assessment procedures are outlined below.

Identify

Person(s) or the situation(s) of concern are identified and reported through the confidential reporting mechanisms or by telling a trusted adult. The BTAM team receives this report and takes *timely* action to conduct a screening by *at least two* of the core team members (school administrator, school psychologist, school counselor, school social worker, school nurse, SRO/LEO).

Inquire

In screening, the BTAM team members must inquire and gather preliminary information to determine if a full assessment is needed. Screening questions include:

1. *Is this an imminent risk situation? Is immediate containment needed by law enforcement (in cases of a threat to others) or mental health (in cases of a threat to self, such as serious suicidal ideations/actions)?*

   - For incidents of harm to others, immediately engage SRO/LEO and/or call 911.
   - For a threat to self, activate emergency mental health protocol and/or call 911.
   - If no to question above, then proceed to question 2.

2. *If a threat is not imminent, does a full threat assessment need to be conducted? Have others expressed concern about this person's behaviors regarding violence or harm to self and/ or others? Has the person threatened violence, engaged in violence, and/or communicated violent intent? Is there a fearful victim or third party?*

- If no to question 2, engage problem solving supports. Document the problem-solving measures taken and close case. No full assessment needed.
- If yes to question 2 and the student does not have a 504 plan or IEP, conduct a full threat assessment.
- If yes question 2 and the student has a 504 plan or IEP, engage 504 coordinator or special education team to determine next steps.
  o If behaviors are consistent with baseline behaviors and can be managed by supports already being received, the BTAM and special education team document problem-solving actions taken and proceeds with current programming.
  o If behaviors are not consistent with baseline behaviors, have escalated, and/or cannot be managed by supports already being received, a full threat assessment needs to be conducted with special education/504 procedures also being followed if changes in programming are warranted.

Note: If BTAM team members are unsure or more information is needed, it is always best to proceed with a full assessment.

Assess

A thorough BTAM assessment includes multi-method, multi-source data collection, assessing risk factors and warning signs, analyzing the data to determine seriousness of threat, and then determining level of concern which informs management.

Data Collection

Data collection is critical as BTAM team decisions are only as good as the thoroughness with which the data is collected. Data must be corroborated as much as possible by collecting multiple data points from a variety of sources. Context must be considered and the interaction among the subject(s) of concern, potential target(s), environmental stressors, and precipitating factors (STEP) can increase or mitigate risk. The graphic below showcases the various types of data to be gathered.

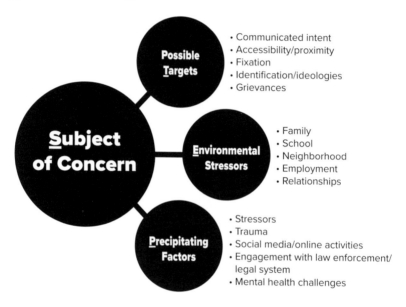

Possible Target(s)

Information regarding the relationship and dynamics between the subject of concern and potential intended target(s) is critical to explore. Targets may be individuals or a specific place. Specific dynamics to explore include:

- Have there been any threats made, directly or indirectly?

- Is the relationship contentious?

- Is the subject fixated on the target with a strong desire to harm?

- Are there specific grievances?

- Has the subject identified with causes/groups/ideologies which perpetuate the desire (and/or provide permission) to harm the intended target(s)?

- Has the intended target(s) rejected or bullied the subject, or has the subject of concern perceived they were rejected or bullied?

- Can the subject gain access to the target(s)?

Environmental Stressors

Environmental and situational stressors are significantly prevalent in most K-12 cases. The recent Secret Service report revealed that almost all of the perpetrators studied had experienced social stressors involving relationships with peers or romantic partners, and nearly all had experienced negative home life factors. Most were victims of bullying, often observed by others (social isolation and exclusion is a form of bullying). A history of school discipline issues and/or contact with law enforcement was also significantly prevalent. Academic challenges were also a contributing factor in some cases. Data regarding environmental stressors include:

- Current and previous academic, mental health, and discipline records, including previous threat and suicide assessments, special education, and 504 records

- Information regarding community, relationship, or employment situations

- Information from law enforcement, probation, juvenile diversion, social services, and/or other involved agencies

- Search of student, student's belongings, locker, car (if applicable) on school property, according to district policy (school officials need reasonable suspicion; law enforcement needs probable cause)

- Search (or search warrant) of room/home/vehicle with law enforcement, if appropriate

- Additional information as determined necessary/helpful

Precipitating Factors

Research has also shown that precipitating factors (stressors), in absence of resiliency and supports, are also a significant contributing factor that can escalate pathway behaviors. Major stressors can include:

- Significant losses (e.g., death/separation from primary caregiver, loss of important relationship)
- Major disappointments (e.g., not achieving a goal)
- Trauma exposure/history of adverse childhood experiences (ACES)
- Social media/online activities that encourage violence, ideation, and/or grievances
- Violent or extreme ideological written and artistic material
- Punitive consequences (in absence of supports also being provided)
- Separation from school (e.g., suspension, expulsion, school breaks)
- Engagement with law enforcement/legal system
- Mental health challenges
- Suicidal ideation
- Coping failures

Presence of mental illness
(but *not* necessarily the driving force behind targeted violence)

Other vulnerabilities, risk factors, stressors, supports

Inhibit or enhance violence concerns and coping

The *perspective* of the subject of concern must be taken into consideration as their perspective (whether based in reality or not) drives behaviors and motives. In addition it is critical most people with mental health ch challenges can make it more difficu good decisions, and maintain emotic challenges *alone* do not cause violen paired with other risk factors, warning direct our attention for engagement of escalation.

Social Media

It is important to verify the origin of social m cases, a student and/or parent established fak accounts and posted threats under another stu student would get kicked out of school. Often the cases involved a parent (or their child) wanting to "eliminate" the competition in an arena such as academics or athletics. Chapter 11 provides an additional resource for digital threat assessment training so adults can identify these types of situations. Such training will also show you how to use social media to gather additional data to inform the threat assessment. SRO/LEOs are also instrumental in helping assess social media communication.

Risk Factors

The intersection of the subject of concern with possible targets, environmental stressors, and precipitating factors must be analyzed, but these are not the only factors to consider. Risk factors, warning signs, and desire to carry out the act must also be considered.

Risk factors increase the probability of a student becoming violent. Risk factors fall into the following categories:

RISK FACTORS FOR TARGETED SCHOOL VIOLENCE	
Problematic Behavioral History	**Mental Health/Health Challenges**
• serious threats of violence • discipline problems • criminal violence • cruelty to animals • intolerance and prejudice • affiliation with gangs	• poor impulse control • uncontrolled anger • impulsive and chronic hitting, intimidating, bullying • mental illness • drug and alcohol use
History/Inappropriate Interest in Violent Behavior	**Social/Environmental Stressors**
• expresses personal grievance moral outrage • thinking framed by extreme ideology • failure to affiliate with prosocial groups • dependent on virtual communities • access to, and/or possession of, firearms • violent expressions in writings and drawings	• socially withdrawn • isolated and alienated • feels rejected • victim of violence/bullying • feels persecuted/picked on • low school interest and performance • occupational goals thwarted

As highlighted before, no set amount of risk factors or formula can predict if an individual will go on to demonstrate warning signs (e.g., pathway behaviors). However, when risk factors interact with STEP factors, the likelihood of warning signs increases.

Warning Signs

Warning signs are concrete indicators that a person of concern is actively considering an act of violence (pathway behaviors). There is no set number of warning signs or a formula that can predict if an individual will act upon the warning signs. Some individuals may be on the pathway for a long time but never reach implementation, and others can escalate quickly. Be sure to direct special attention to the individual expressing suicidal thoughts, as these are often paired with homicidal thoughts. A suicide risk assessment must also be conducted.

WARNING SIGNS FOR TARGETED SCHOOL VIOLENCE	
Pathway Behaviors	Emotional Despair

• Ideation
  o articulates motives: personal, political, religious, racial/ethnic, environmental, special interest
• Planning
  o targets identified
  o plan developed
  o leakage of ideations
• Preparation/Acquisition
  o gains access to weapons/ methods of planned harm
  o practicing/refining plan
• Implementation
  o time-imperative actions that demonstrate act will be carried out soon
	• social withdrawal
	• emotional state: hopelessness, helplessness, desperation, despair
	• suicidal thinking/ideation
	• anger/hopelessness from feeling picked on, teased, bullied, humiliated, rejected
	• increasing capacity to carry out threats
	• intimate partner problems
	• interpersonal conflicts
	• significant losses (relationships, supports, life situation)
	• personal failures
	• victims of abuse/toxic stressors

Identifying with Previous Acts of Violence	Fixation
• engagement with social media/ internet sites/other persons facilitating or promoting violence • research of previous acts of violence to refine own plan	• increasing intensity of violence related to efforts, desires, planning • words consistent with actions • sees violence as acceptable/only solution

Sources: Amman et al. (2017); de Becker (n.d.); Fein et al. (2004); Langman (2009, 2015); Meloy et al., (2011, 2014, 2015); Nicoletti & Spencer (2002); Reeves & Brock (2017).

To help gather the critical information described above, a thorough records review and direct, matter of fact, non-judgmental interviews should take place with the individual of concern, parent/guardian, school staff, potential target(s) of threat, and others who may have information. Interviews gather information not always captured by observations or records, and often lead to additional data sources.

Trauma-Informed Assessment

As mentioned previously, stress levels for both students and adults have increased exponentially over the past year. Thus, is it important to conduct a trauma-informed assessment[23] and assess the personal impact of recent and past events.

1. How has the pandemic impacted you?

2. How has social distancing impacted you?

3. What activities are you currently engaged with (social, academic, extra-curricular, etc.)?

4. What racial bias, tension, and inequities have you experienced?

5. What systematic racism and implicit racism have you experienced?

6. What racial tension and inequities have you witnessed?

7. How are you coping with daily stressors?

8. Have you experienced hopelessness?

9. Have you had suicidal thoughts?

10. How are you doing academically?

11. What supports do you have socially? At home? Virtually?

12. What coping mechanism has been working well for you?

Determining Imminence and Intent

The TOADS acronym[24] helps to facilitate conversations and data collection to determine imminence and intent.

Time	Time to execute their plan? If time imperative, immediate containment is needed by mental health or law enforcement custody.
Opportunity	Opportunity to carry out the plan and/or able to access targets?
Ability	Ability (cognitive, physical, and developmental) to carry out plan?
Desire	Desire to carry out plan? Grievances, anger, retaliation, despair, etc. Sees no other option besides violence.
Stimulus	Negative stressor(s) that serves as stimulus/trigger for carrying out the harmful act.

As each variable above increases in the affirmative, risk and concern increases.

Galvin de Becker[25] uses the acronym JACA:

Justification	Strong justification for wanting to harm self and/or others?
Alternatives	Willing to consider any alternatives besides violence?
Consequences	Cares about the consequences of their actions?
Ability	Ability to carry act out?

A strong justification and ability to carry out a violent act increases risk. If willing to consider other non-violent alternatives, concerned about the consequences, and willing to engage with supports, these are positive signs that help to mitigate risk.

Analyzing the Data

Wanting to conduct an act of violence results from a complex interaction between the subject(s), target(s), environment, precipitating events, risk factors, warning signs, and contextual and developmental factors.

The U.S. Secret Service best practice guidelines highly recommend analyzing the data according to eleven key investigative questions. BTAM team members should engage in a group discussion after *all* data is collected to answer the questions below.

1. What are the person's motives and goals?

2. Have there been any communications suggesting ideas or intent to attack or harm others?

3. Has the person shown inappropriate interest in previous attacks, weapons, incidents of mass violence, and/or is the person engaged in obsessive pursuit, stalking, or monitoring of intended victims?

4. Has the person engaged in attack-related behaviors (i.e., planning; any behavior that moves an idea of harm toward actual harm)?

5. Does the person have the capacity to carry out an act of targeted violence?

6. Is the person experiencing hopelessness, desperation, and/or despair?

7. Does the person have a trusting relationship with at least one responsible person (e.g., a teacher, family member, coach, counselor, advisor)?

8. Does the person see violence as an acceptable, desirable, or only way to solve problems?

9. Are the person's conversation and story consistent with his or her actions?

10. Are other people concerned about the person's potential for violence?

11. What circumstances might affect the likelihood of violence—either increase it or decrease it (stressors and/or protective factors)?

If there is evidence of suicidal ideation, a suicide risk assessment must also be conducted. Additional guidance analyzing each of the eleven questions above can be found in the downloadable resources.

Predatory/Planned vs. Impulsive/Reactive Violence

In addition to criteria listed above, threat assessment literature has identified two primary types of targeted violence. These are important to understand as they can impact the analysis of motives and intent and can guide management.

Predatory/planned behaviors are:

- premeditated, planned, and purposeful
- individual shows minimal emotion or expression
- violence is directed against specified targets and has a purpose or goal, often to fulfill a grievance
- plans are often detailed and very attack-oriented (but subject does not necessarily share plan with others)
- not time limited—can be on the pathway for a long time (and possibly never escalate to implementation) or might escalate quickly under the right combination of stressors or motives

For many people displaying predatory/planned violence, vengeance and notoriety is what they want, suicidal intent is often present, and copycats are a concern because of the magnitude of their actions and the notoriety they often get. The predatory and planned violence can be hard to detect as potential perpetrators often keep intentions hidden. Intervention is more difficult with these individuals as they justify their actions based upon their own worldview. Some may also exhibit anti-social and/or narcissistic qualities. While interventions can help, early identification, management, and careful supervision is key.

Impulsive/reactive behaviors are:

- reactive (emotion-based) and immediate
- often in response to a perceived threat
- goal is threat reduction; reactions are emotional or defensive in nature
- time limited—if the perceived or real threat is minimized/not present, they do not feel an on-ongoing need to lash out or harm

Trauma responses can often manifest themselves in impulsive/reactive threatening behaviors. The impulsive/reactive type of violence is often already on a BTAM team's radar because the person often exhibits externalizing behaviors and emotions when threatened or provoked. This type also includes individuals who have significant trauma histories and exposure to toxic stressors (i.e., adverse childhood experiences—ACEs).

Therefore, it is critical that trauma responses are recognized as such and not misinterpreted as a threat. Another book in this same 15-Minute Focus series titled *Trauma and Adverse Childhood Experiences* is a must-read for becoming more trauma-informed. It explains how trauma impacts behavior, with a focus on how to proactively intervene and manage behaviors. If we can decrease the perceived or real threat (i.e., stressors), help teach emotional regulation and coping skills, and engage mental health supports, we are often successful in helping these individuals move onto a more positive pathway.

Students with Special Needs

Care and caution are needed when conducting a threat assessment involving a student with special needs. School professionals (i.e., school psychologists) who are specially trained in diagnosing and working with students with special needs must be engaged in the process. There are too many stories of students with special needs being suspended or placed in more restrictive placements for *making* a threat but not *posing* a threat. For example, students on the autism spectrum have language and social deficits. They often mimic specific phrases, act out behaviors they have seen in movies or videos, or make comments without understanding how they may be interpreted by others. Those with intellectual disabilities may say or do things without understanding the meaning of their works or actions. Those with disabilities can also have periods of emotional or sensorial dysregulation. They can become overwhelmed by sensorial input or someone being in their personal space; they can be hypersensitive to cues (e.g., teacher raising their voice) and have "melt downs" as a result. In addition, they may not have the advanced reasoning skills to realize when a social media post or behavior is inappropriate, scary, or dangerous. A BTAM team rushing to judgment without thoughtful analysis of the threat and how the disability may impact intent only contributes to disproportionality in discipline. And if a management decision is removal from their least restrictive environment, the BTAM team may be violating IDEA (Individuals with Disabilities Education Act). The context, social-emotional and cognitive development, and disability must all be carefully considered before any management decisions are made. The following additional questions should be asked when assessing threats involving students with special needs:

1. Is this student reacting to a perceived threat (e.g., person invaded their personal space, person made a demanding request without warning that it would be time to transition activities, sensorial overload, trauma trigger—startling sound/noise)?

2. Was this the result of a skills deficit (i.e., social skills) or in response to a peer conflict that could be resolved through problem-solving (i.e., teach the student how to politely ask for more personal space in line or how to politely ask how to join the game)?

3. Does this student have the cognitive ability to understand their actions and their impact on others?

4. Does this student have the cognitive and/or physical capabilities to plan and acquire the means to carry out an act of violence?

5. Does this student have a behavior plan to proactively address escalation?

6. Did the adults contribute to the escalation due to a lack of training in de-escalation and/or lack of training in specialized approaches needed? Could escalation have been prevented if handled differently?

7. Is this a report of threat to comfort (i.e., "this student is weird") versus an actual threat to safety (i.e., pathway behaviors are evident)?

Most cases involving students with special needs result from them making a threat, not posing a threat (making it a low-level concern). If this is the case, problem solving, teaching of replacement behaviors, establishment of a good behavior intervention plan that focuses on preventing escalation, and integrating good behavior management and trauma-informed strategies are appropriate. The use of overly punitive management strategies can be harmful.

Determine Level of Concern

After ALL data is analyzed and the key questions are answered, the BTAM team must determine a level(s) of concern (as outlined by the FBI). Again, there is no mathematical formula or specific number of risk factors and warning signs that determine a specific level of concern, and the levels are not predictive of human behavior. Levels of concern help to guide and ensure that appropriate interventions are recommended based upon the level of concern.

For example, suspension or expulsion should not be utilized for a low-level concern. Levels of concern should not automatically determine a change of educational placement. Data gathered in the BTAM process may be used in evaluating programmatic changes, but the threat assessment process does not replace the due process needed for a change in placement or programming.

The following explanation of levels of concern is adapted from guidance provided by the FBI[26] and is offered as general guidance to conceptualize each level. More specific guidance is offered in the downloadable resources (see Table of Contents for more info). When determining the level of concern, focus should not be on checking specific boxes at a certain level. Some individuals may show indictors of one level of concern (i.e., moderate level for risk of harming others) but because parents refuse to acknowledge concerns or put supports in place, this individual is a high risk for potential escalation and needing intensive monitoring and supervision. The actions taken by the team after analyzing the data is important.

Low level concern	Individual/situation does not appear to pose a threat of violence or serious harm to self/others; any exhibited issues/concerns can be resolved through problem-solving measures; threat often stated out of frustration/anger; disability impacts ability to understand how words/actions are perceived by others; existing supports in place can effectively manage concerns
Moderate level concern	Person/situation does not appear to pose a threat of violence, or serious harm to self/others at this time, but exhibits some behaviors that indicate potential intent for future violence or serious harm to self/others if stressors are not minimized; exhibits other concerning behaviors that require intervention; open to engaging accessible supports
High level concern	Person/situation appears to pose a threat of violence, is exhibiting behaviors that indicate a continuing intent to harm, has made efforts to acquire means and/or has capacity and desire to carry out plan; may also exhibit other concerning behaviors that require immediate interventions to mitigate risk; some resistance to engaging supports or time needed to engage supports; intensive monitoring and supervision is needed
Imminent concern	Person/situation poses a clear and immediate threat of serious violence toward others that requires immediate containment actions (law enforcement or mental health hold/admission) to protect self and identifiable target(s).

Two key questions guide actions to take after determining level of concern:

1. Does the subject pose a threat of violence to others and/or self?

2. Does the student need additional interventions and **ongoing** supports and engagement for a period of time to mitigate risk, decrease stressors, and build protective factors?

If "NO" to both (i.e., low risk) then:

- Document the BTAM process followed and actions taken to resolve the concern.

- If the subject could benefit from school-based or community interventions or supports, provide appropriate resources and referrals; document these referrals.

- Close the case or place on inactive status

If "YES" to question 1 or 2, (i.e., moderate, high, imminent) then:

- Take appropriate actions.

- Develop an intervention, supervision, and monitoring plan, appropriate for level of risk.

- Provide school-based interventions and community referrals and supports.

- Document the case, including referrals made.

- Assign a case manager for progress monitoring, accountability, and follow-up.

The greater the concern, the more directive and intensive the supports and management plan must be.

Case Study (Sarah)

While Sarah communicated intent to harm, it was impulsive and reactive, a passing thought in the moment, and there was no true intent to harm. There was no evidence of risk factors, warning signs, or environmental or situational stressors, and no evidence of other concerning behaviors, mental health challenges, or pathway behaviors. When law enforcement showed up at her house, she was scared and remorseful and engaged in conversation about the seriousness of her actions and the negative outcomes that could result. She was apologetic and willing to problem solve, but the administrator did not give her the opportunity because he took a zero-tolerance approach to Sarah making a threat. Sarah was low risk.

Case Study (Jordan)

Jordan was initially resistant to talking with the school counselor when she began the threat assessment interview. After acknowledging that the past months had been very difficult, Jordan began to open up about life at home. Jordan's dad was recently arrested for dealing drugs, mom has been drinking again, and brother has run away and is "out of control." Access to internet has been inconsistent, making it hard to keep up with school, and there had been little to no interaction with peers the past few months. Jordan acknowledged making the statements and admitted to being angry with those who "seem to have it all and couldn't care less about what anyone else is going through." Jordan admitted to having thoughts of wanting to harm others and had even begun to assemble a general plan, admitting the basketball game would be the easiest time and place to harm others. Jordan did not have specific details and denied access to means, but expressed hopelessness and despair due to lost hope the family situation would ever change. Teachers also reported changes in behaviors and emotions as Jordan became more despondent and less engaged. They actually had Jordan on the list to discuss at their next student intervention team meeting. When asked about supports, Jordan denied having any supportive family members but identified the school counselor, school psychologist, and English teacher as those who care. Jordan wants help and seemed relieved to be having this discussion, but Jordan was not sure what anyone could do. When Jordan's mom was contacted, she reluctantly came to school and while relatively cooperative, she demonstrated little energy to engage supports or increase monitoring and supervision. The SRO confirmed the family information was true. Patrol officers had been monitoring Jordan's home to be sure Jordan and mom were safe from dealers trying to collect money. The BTAM team felt that Jordan was a moderate risk for harming others but could potentially escalate to high risk if family stressors were not mitigated and supports not put in place.

Special Needs Case Study (Blake)

Blake is an eighth-grade student with autism. When the teaching assistant told Blake to turn off the computer game, Blake failed to comply immediately. The assistant grabbed the game out of Blake's hands. Blake escalated by knocking over a desk and running through the hallway screaming, "I'm going to kill her," while making stabbing motions in the air with the pencil. Students overheard the commotion and one student reported to a teacher "that a classmate was running through the hallway threatening to kill other students." Other students started texting their parents with the same (inaccurate) information. The assistant principal, SRO, school psychologist, and school counselor were called in. They were able to use de-escalation strategies to get Blake into the main office. They began the threat assessment process by talking with Blake, the teaching assistant, classroom teacher, and witnesses in the hallway. In analyzing the data, they determined this was reactive in nature. Blake was mad at the assistant for grabbing the game. While Blake acknowledged that it is bad to say you want to kill someone, Blake did not fully understand the consequences of saying those words. There was no evidence of ongoing ideation or desire to hurt the assistant and no evidence of a plan. Due to careful engagement and monitoring of adults at home, and Blake's lower cognitive ability, the BTAM team determined that it was unlikely that Blake could gather means to kill the assistant. When interviews were conducted of students in the hallway, they stated that Blake never stabbed anyone, nor did Blake go after anyone. They said that Blake was "weird" at times, but they had never felt threatened by Blake. They had known Blake to escalate only when overwhelmed, unexpected transitions occurred, or Blake's personal space in invaded. Other staff also verified the accounts and perspectives. Blake made a threat but did not pose a threat. This was a low-risk concern best handled via problem solving and better staff training.

QUESTIONS to CONSIDER

1. What barriers to data collection could occur? How would your team address this barrier?

2. How have trauma and stress impacted your students? How would you assess what interventions and supports are needed?

3. How would your team approach analyzing the data, according to the Secret Service questions?

4. What protocols and/or training are needed to ensure considerationsregardingstudents with special needs are integrated in your team's process?

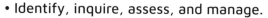

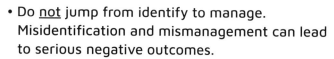

KEY POINTS

- Identify, inquire, assess, and manage.
- Do <u>not</u> jump from identify to manage. Misidentification and mismanagement can lead to serious negative outcomes.
- Multi-method, multi-source, trauma-informed, comprehensive data collection must be conducted and information verified.
- Targeted violence is a complex interaction of multiple factors.
- Level of concern and management strategies are a team decision.

Developing Risk Management Options

Step 6

Management is just as critical as the assessment; punishment alone does not change behavior. This critical question is: *How can we intervene to help the individual off the pathway to violence and onto a more positive pathway?*

Some people erroneously believe that punishment will stop behavior, or that suspending or expelling a student will decrease the threat risk once the individual is removed from their environment. Unfortunately, that is not the case. Even if suspension (or expulsion) is used, most often those students return and schools are obligated to provide educational services. While punishment may temporarily suppress negative behaviors, those same behaviors are more likely to resurface unless adults teach positive replacement behaviors, engage supports, or address the mental health and/or situational stressors. Disconnecting the person of concern from monitoring and supports can further escalate emotions and grievances and only shifts the potential threat to the community. A recent analysis of K-12 school shootings[27] showed that 41 percent of school attacks took place within the first week back to school following a break in attendance (i.e., suspension, school holidays, absence due to illness or truancy). Twenty-four percent of the attacks took place on the first day the attacker returned to school after an absence, and in two incidents the attacker was suspended from school at the time of the attack. This underlines the importance of implementing consequences only after careful team consideration, and these consequences should always be paired with supportive interventions. For example, mitigation may best be done by *not* suspending the student of concern and keeping them at school in order to implement interventions and supports. This increases connectedness and supervision and decreases the opportunity for them to be at home alone, which increases time available to conduct research, plan, and carry-out an attack. Successful management is highly dependent on appropriate interventions and supports being put in place.

Levels of Concern

Interventions must be appropriate to the level of concern and paired with messages of care and concern. Supports are put in place to learn from this experience, and goals are established so offenders can earn their way back to the general education setting or meet a newly established goal (e.g., graduating from the alternative high school to pursue post-secondary education/employment).

Below is general guidance on appropriate interventions based upon level of concern. Additional guidance is provided in the downloadable resources.

- *Low levels* of concern can be handled through problem solving, conflict resolution, and if needed, engaging Tier 2 supports in school. Use the situation as a learning opportunity and help the individual understand why choosing better ways to convey their frustration, anger, disappointment, humor, etc. is more beneficial. School and community supports may also be recommended (i.e., mentoring program).

- *Moderate levels* of concern can be addressed by engaging Tier 2 supports, involving school mental and behavioral health professionals (see chapter 9), increasing intensity of interventions, and collaborating with parents and possibly community supports.

- *High levels* of concern include all the above, but programming and supports become much more structured and intensive with a formal intervention plan being established with ongoing progress monitoring. Community supports are often engaged, or if parent refuses recommended school and/or community supports, this refusal should be documented.

- *Imminent* concerns require engagement of law enforcement and/or community mental health, because containment is likely needed due to imminent safety concerns. Sharing of information and collaborative programming between the school, family, and community agencies/professionals is needed to help direct the individual off the pathway to violence.

As emphasized earlier, the levels of concern are not predictive of behavior; they guide BTAM teams on how directive and intensive any interventions need to be. For example, suspension should not be utilized for low-level concern and is even questionable to use for a moderate level concern. Expulsion should never be used for a low or moderate level concern.

Interventions, management, and supports are a *team* decision. Different perspectives need to be taken into consideration, with the pros and cons of each decision and unintended consequences considered, before any final decisions are made.

Multi-Tiered Systems of Supports

As introduced in chapter 3, proactively building resiliency and protective safeguards for the students by engaging multi-tiered systems of supports and resources helps to establish a safe school climate and mitigates escalation of behaviors. When implemented with fidelity a positive school climate and culture establishes a strong foundation for effective BTAM. Specific guidance includes:

- A culture that emphasizes positive communication, acceptance and inclusion, where diversity is celebrated
- A clean and positive physical environment
- Character education/consistent school values
- School curriculum and organizational norms that promote the development of fundamental values in children
- Social-emotional learning (SEL) curriculum that emphases self-awareness, self-management, social awareness, relationship skills, and responsible decision making
- School-wide positive discipline program with student engagement to help establish and support expectations
- Consistent and equitable rule enforcement
- Programs and opportunities that build adult-student relationships (e.g., mentoring, activity clubs)
- Positive office referrals/recognition— "Caught You Caring." Positive reinforcement for positive behaviors (e.g., attendance, being on time, improving grades, helping others, being a good role model, meeting behavior goals)
- Increased parent involvement and positive communication regarding their child's accomplishments and growth
- Systematic screening programs for early identification and intervention (e.g., school climate and safety, mental health, bullying, suicide)
- Mediation programs, including peer mediation
- Bullying prevention and intervention programs for both bullies and victims; emphasis on students being "up-standers" (reporting concerns and supporting those being bullied)
- Conflict de-escalation training that teaches staff and students to recognize and disengage from escalating conflict

- Trauma-informed practices such as trauma-informed/ trauma-sensitive schools

In addition to focusing on climate and culture, effective management strategies include interventions that focus on monitoring, relationship building, skills development/resiliency building, and discipline.

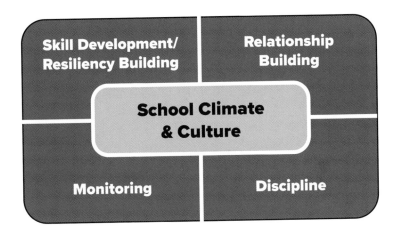

Appendix B provides a detailed list of interventions, supports, and resources to consider. A resource mapping tool, provided in the downloadable resources, should be utilized to identify current resources available for effective management. Resources should be updated regularly and attention should be directed to continuously enhancing intervention supports available.

Alternatives to Suspension

Research has shown the over-representation of some minority groups in regard to the use of suspension and expulsion.[28] In addition, IDEA (Individual with Disabilities Education Act) and case law have indicated that long-term suspension or expulsion can violate the Free Appropriate Public Education (FAPE) guarantee for students with disabilities. Research also shows that suspension and expulsion do not change behavior or deter others. Instead, it can actually contribute to a decrease in academic progress and an increase in drop-out rates and negative life outcomes.[29] Thus, alternatives to suspension must be utilized.

Alternatives to suspension can include:

Restorative practices	Emphasizes inclusiveness, relationship-building, and problem-solving, through restorative methods (e.g., restorative circles) that bring victims, offenders, and their supports together to address wrongdoing; students reflect upon and take responsibility for their actions and identify solutions to repair harm.
Problem solving	Teach effective steps to problem solving; include modeling and practicing.
Contracting	Includes reinforcers for success and consequences for continuing problem behaviors
Mini-courses or skill modules	Assign mini-courses or self-study modules as a disciplinary consequence related to inappropriate behavior. Teach increased awareness and strategies that facilitate behavior change (e.g., anger control, conflict resolution; anxiety management; social skills).
Counseling or mentoring	In-school and/or out of school
Parent involvement, collaboration, and supervision	Invite parents to brainstorm ideas for better home-school collaboration and communication, and coordinate behavior-change approaches and reinforcements for progress seen at home and school.
Behavior support / intervention plan	Focus on replacing inappropriate behaviors by teaching replacement behaviors, and increasing and rewarding desirable behaviors (e.g., self-charting of behaviors, reinforcers, feedback sessions)

Appropriate in-school suspension	In-school suspension should include academic tutoring, mini-courses or skill modules focused on skill-building related to the concerns, and a clearly defined procedure for returning to class contingent on student progress or behavior.
	Caution: Ensure in-school suspension is not used to avoid attending class; appropriate management of the in-school suspension environment is needed.
Alternative programming*	Provide short- or long-term changes in student's schedule, classes, or course content. Programming should be tailored to student needs. Change of placement or programming must be made by the IEP (Individualized Education Program) team if student receives special education services.
Community service	Engage in an activity that allows them to show positive growth, build connections, and develop empathy for others.

* To reiterate: Alternative programming should NOT be use as a babysitting service or to remove a student because of pressure from other stakeholders. Misuse or overuse of alternative programming disrupts the learning environment for those students who truly need and benefit from the alternative program.

Expulsion Hearing

The BTAM process is not an expulsion hearing. BTAM data may be used to help determine if expulsion is appropriate, but due process proceedings for expulsion must still be followed. The team needs to carefully consider the consequences of further disconnecting the individual from academic supports and engagement.

Special Education

Completion of a threat assessment does not automatically necessitate a referral for special education or a change in placement. A special education referral would only occur if the student legitimately could meet qualification criteria for one of the thirteen disability categories and specialized instructional services are needed to meet their needs. Over-referral of threat assessment cases to special education programs can have a significant negative impact on those students who legitimately qualify and need those services.

If the student of concern is receiving special education services, special education policies and procedures must still be followed. The BTAM assessment is not a manifestation determination review (MDR). While BTAM assessment data may be used in an MDR, the MDR meeting and process must still occur. If a change in programming is determined to be appropriate, an IEP Review and the change of placement process must still be followed.

Managing Fear

- Potential targets might be understandably alarmed, especially if the threat circulates over social media, which further increases concerns. Actions may need to be taken to manage fear:

- Ensure your technology specialist, social media specialist, and/or public information officer (PIO) are monitoring the publicly accessible social media sites.

- If needed, PIO may need to disseminate a general message stating that the school is aware of the situation, the appropriate intervention team has been engaged, the situation is being assessed, and protective actions are being taken.

- Provide a reminder to potential target(s) that there are legal limitations to the specifics of what can be shared but that safety is of utmost priority. Request that they avoid contributing to public dissemination of information (i.e., getting on social media to share concerns) as this can escalate stressors for the individual of concern; avoid rumors and direct them where to find factual information.

- Suggest potential targets(s) reduce social media presence, creating less ability for the person making the threat to interact. This may involve activating privacy settings, turning off location trackers, and engaging other protective safeguards.

- Ask friends and family members to stop indicating or "tagging" the potential target in social media posts and pictures. This means turning off tagging and geotracking options.

- Work with teachers to ensure intended targets are not placed into classrooms or group assignments with the individuals displaying potential threatening behaviors.

- Continue to dialogue with potential targets(s) and address their concerns.

Documentation

According to the Family Educational Rights and Privacy Act (FERPA), disciplinary action may be kept in student records if the behavior posed a significant risk to the safety and well-being of that student, other students, or staff. However, "significant" is not operationally defined. As such, there is little legal guidance on the development, storage, and retention of threat assessment records for behaviors that do not reach that threshold. It is important for each district/school to obtain guidance from legal counsel in regard to the management of threat assessment records. Decisions on record keeping are important. Maintaining records helps to establish a legal and behavioral justification for intervention and counter claims of negligence. The documentation must be thorough enough to demonstrate the actions taken by the BTAM team to support their good faith efforts to identify, inquire, assess, and manage threatening situations. Efforts attempted and limitations should also be noted. Schools may not have the legal authority to access certain types of information (e.g., counseling records from a private mental health clinician) but efforts to obtain a signed release of information must be documented. Documentation of progress monitoring and follow-up supports is also critical to demonstrate ongoing engagement until the concern has been resolved or the student graduates.

BTAM records must also be maintained as long as allowed under relevant laws or regulations, as individuals may pose an ongoing threat after leaving school, graduating, or losing employment. At minimum, there should be a consistent process for confidential record-keeping at each school. There should also be consistent guidelines for when and how the records are shared when a student transitions between schools or moves outside of the school. A copy of the completed BTAM protocol should also be sent to a district-level coordinator/administrator. This ensures that the process is being done with fidelity, and it creates a back-up record in case the record needs to be referenced in the future. It also allows for the gathering of statistics to inform strategic investment of future BTAM resources. If records are stored electronically, security compliance (i.e., HIPAA, FERPA, privacy laws pertaining to electronic storage of records) must be adhered to.

Parent Cooperation and Refusal

Parents are partners in this process, so no level of risk should be determined until parents have been interviewed and engaged in a collaborative process. Their level of engagement, cooperation, and acknowledgment of concerns can impact level of concern. Their perspective is critical, and we must talk *with* them, not at them. Parents' emotions and behavior can escalate quickly (i.e., "lawyer up") if they feel the decision has been made before they have been heard and their perspective considered. If this is viewed as a collaborative process, parents feel safer to be truthful and engage recommended supports.

What if a parent refuses to cooperate with the assessment or refuses recommended interventions and supports? Document, document, document! If there is a high or imminent concern for safety, report to child protective services and/or law enforcement and document that action. Parent refusal does not exempt the school from conducting the BTAM assessment and implementing as many interventions, monitoring, and supports as needed and legally allowed without parent cooperation.

Progress Monitoring and Staying Engaged

For each situation, a case manager must be identified to ensure:

- all appropriate paperwork is completed and stored in the designated location

- persons with a legitimate need to know are notified of any change in status

- intervention referrals are made, and follow through or lack of follow through by parent/guardian is documented

- additional concerning information that is cause for a reassessment or change in programming is shared with the team

For subjects determined to be low risk, informal monitoring may be sufficient. If determined to be moderate, high, or imminent risk, more formalized progress monitoring should be implemented for a period of time until the student is no longer a concern for violence. Follow-up meetings should be scheduled to review progress with adjustments made as needed. When formal monitoring is no longer needed (due to a positive response to interventions) and the person no longer poses a safety concern, the case can be closed or placed on inactive status. However, if ongoing supports are needed, the student should stay engaged with the BTAM team or another intervention team.

Case Study (Sarah)

Sarah's case (see previous chapters) could have been handled with problem-solving, an apology, and restorative practices. Sarah could have remained at school and Heather would not have been ostracized by peers. The "zero tolerance" approach used by the untrained school administrator had serious negative consequences for both students. This could have been avoided if a team process had been used.

Case Study (Jordan)

Jordan needed intensive supports, both at home and at school. School supports included the following:

- The school administrator used a problem-solving process to discuss the seriousness of these statements. They also discussed Jordan's passion for helping those from diverse cultures. Jordan joined the school's diversity club, which allowed for engagement in positive leadership and advocacy.

- The English teacher provided mentoring.

- Tutoring supports were implemented.

- Progress monitoring was conducted by the school student intervention team.

- Jordan needed to obtain prior permission to attend after-school activities, with increased supervision provided by staff.

- His mom agreed to let the SRO search the home (no weapons found).

- SRO and patrol officers monitored the home situation closely with increased patrols.

- The school administrator and mental health team conducted a universal screening with all students that assessed social-emotional well-being, school climate, and culture; Jordan was not the only student showing signs of stress.

Case Study (Blake)

Blake earned a checkmark (negative consequence) on his daily behavior chart for running out of class and yelling in the hallway. His teacher integrated social stories about following teacher directions, why there are limits to game time, and how to use the cool-down spot. SEL lessons were conducted on how to appropriately express anger and frustration. The assistant teacher received additional training on providing a five-minute prompt before requesting Blake transition, and how to verbally de-escalate Blake.

- The school administrator sent a message to parents clarifying the facts. He stated that there was an upset student in the hallway and the situation was addressed. He also stated that contrary to information parents or others may have seen on social media, there was no threat of harm and this student did not come into any physical contact with other students.

Mental health supports for Jordan and Blake are discussed in chapter 9.

QUESTIONS to CONSIDER

1. Conduct the resource mapping exercise found in the downloadable resources. What were the results? How can intervention options be enhanced or improved?

2. How will your team document any cases of potential violence? Store records?

3. What is the communication protocol if threats become public knowledge and parents demand to know the specifics of a threat and how the school is responding?

KEY POINTS

- Punishment alone does not change behavior.
- Replacement skills must be taught and engaging supports must take place to increase likelihood of long-term positive changes.
- Develop a list of resources and supports (resource mapping) to guide intervention and support planning.
- Interventions selected must match level of concern.
- Document, document, document!

Role of Administrators & Collaboration with SROs and School Mental Health Professionals

Well-trained BTAM administrators are critical to the BTAM process. Administrators who have not been trained and/or have the mindset of punishment are counter-productive to the process and might even put their school at greater risk.

School Climate

Administrators are the key to establishing and modeling a positive school climate. They set the tone. If universal programming has a strong focus on building positive, trusting relationships with one another, individuals will be more comfortable bringing concerns forward. Administrator must be visible, approachable, and trusted to handle reported threats responsibly. Relationships are the #1 prevention and mitigation tool to school violence.

Leadership

Administrative leadership and engagement are critical to the BTAM process, as the "buck stops" with the administrator. Administrators:

- respond to reported concerns in a timely manner
- provide positive leadership and guidance during the process
- are responsible for ensuring team members follow through on their BTAM duties
- hold staff accountable for implementation of interventions and supports
- ensure equitable and fair practices

Failure to do the things above could result in claims of negligence. After action reports and analyses regarding the Marjory Stoneman Douglas and Arapahoe High School shootings, both criticized administrators for not being more involved in the threat assessment process that was conducted prior to the shootings being carried out. The Bowe Cleveland v. Taft Union High School District (CA) lawsuit, among the first school shooting-related lawsuits to go to trial and result in a monetary award for the student plaintiff, also found a lack of engagement and response to concerns by administrators. In all three cases above, claims were made that the threat assessment process was not done thoroughly and the interventions and management plans were insufficient.

Collaboration and Communication

How administrators approach threat assessment sets the tone for either a supportive, intervention-focused process, or one that can become argumentative and punishment-focused. When conducting stakeholder training on the BTAM process, administrators need to convey that safety is of utmost importance, and threats will be taken seriously and acted upon quicky. Emphasis should be placed on how the BTAM process is focused on helping individuals address challenges and onto a more positive pathway.

Administrators need to:

- build positive relationships with parents, student, and community partners
- educate school community about safety initiatives and supports, the BTAM process, and confidential reporting mechanisms
- emphasize the importance of reporting concerns
- communicate ongoing message of "safety is everyone's responsibility"
- respond to threatening concerns in a matter of fact, non-emotional manner; consult with public information officer on appropriate messaging
- balance confidentiality of individuals with communicating steps being taken to address concerns
- engage parents in a problem-solving process

Management/Intervention Decisions

Administrators must avoid jumping to management too quickly or making management decisions on their own. A thorough assessment must be conducted before any management and intervention decisions are made. While punitive outcomes may be necessary, particularly if a law or district conduct code has been violated and there is no flexibility to decide consequences (e.g., bringing a weapon on campus by law results in expulsion), the punitive actions must be paired with interventions and support services (i.e., "consequences with care"). If the student feels like "the rug has been pulled out from under them" or they are being "thrown aside" or used as the "fall guy," emotions and grievances can lead to pathway escalation. To prevent escalation of pathway behaviors, consideration of alternatives to suspension and implementing consequences with care are critical.

Utilization of School Mental Health Professionals

School mental health professionals (school psychologists, school counselors, school social workers) have critical experience, education, and skills to help provide interventions and supports to those at-risk. However, their skills are often underutilized because administrators do not understand or value their expertise with mental health and behavior. Some administrators erroneously believe mental health services are not the responsibility of schools or are better provided by community professionals. These myths and misperceptions need to be debunked.

School psychologists have expertise and training in the following ten domain areas: 1) data-based decision making, 2) consultation and collaboration, 3) academic interventions and supports, 4) mental and behavioral health services, 5) school-wide practices to promote learning, 6) services to promote safe and supportive schools, 7) family, school, and community collaboration, 8) equitable practices for diverse populations, 9) research and evidenced-based practices, and 10) legal, ethical, and professional practice. However, they are most often used for special education eligibility testing. Administrators need to broaden the job description and use school psychologists' expertise to: establish and evaluate universal prevention programs focusing on school climate; analyze the functions of behavior to help establish high quality behavior intervention, supervision, and support plans; and to provide school-based mental health interventions; all which contribute to effective management.

School counselors are often relegated to test coordination and scheduling. Administrators must allow them to use their expertise in delivering mental health interventions, supporting positive connections and school climate, and helping a student plan for a positive future. Similarly, school social workers should be providing mental health supports, working with parents to ensure family stressors are addressed, and making sure parenting and community supports are engaged. In short, effective administrators maximize the talents of their school mental health professionals. See chapter 10 for additional information.

Partnering with Law Enforcement

Law enforcement officers (LEOs) are critical partners in preventing and mitigating risk of violence. School resource officers, when carefully selected and properly trained in the unique aspects of school policing, are critical to school safety and building positive relationships. The mission of the National Association of School Resource Officers (NASRO) is to "provide the highest quality of training to school-based law enforcement officers to promote safer schools and safer children." While there has been a lot of discussion and research regarding the school-to-prison pipeline, proper training and use of SROs actually helps *prevent* the school-to-prison pipeline. Due to the unique environment and populations served in schools, NASRO strongly advocates for the following:

- SROs must be carefully selected and properly trained to work in the school setting in the proper use of police powers and authority in a school environment. NASRO offers basic and advanced SRO training courses[30] focusing on positive, proactive school policing practices.

- SRO roles are clearly defined and include three primary roles: 1) law enforcement officer, 2) teacher, and 3) informal counselor

- The primary focus of SROs is on proactive school policing with a strong emphasis on relationship building and de-escalation of concerning behaviors.

- Limit SRO involvement in formal school discipline. SRO involvement in disciplinary actions should only be used if immediate physical containment is needed due to an imminent physical safety risk (i.e., weapon on campus).[31] SROs are not to be engaged in school discipline.

- A memorandum of understanding (MOU) should be signed by law enforcement agency and head of the educational institution agreeing to items above. Administrators and SROs should work closely together.

The following are additional duties of an SRO:

- Engage in school activities

- Set a positive and engaging climate

- Serve on school safety/crisis team and BTAM team

- Help develop safety plan and protocols

- Monitor safety and build connections with students and staff during passing periods, lunch, school drop-off and pickup, and school events

- Teach safety lessons (drug and alcohol awareness, gang prevention, personal safety, motor vehicle safety, crime prevention)

- Co-teach SEL lessons with teachers and/or school mental health professionals

- Mentor at-risk students

- Help students' problem-solve and engage in peaceful conflict resolution

- Report patterns of escalating behaviors/concerns to school leaders/intervention teams to engage proactive supports before escalation

- Attend problem-solving/intervention team meetings to contribute ideas for interventions and supports

- Facilitate home-school-community partnerships

- Help provide increased supervision and monitoring, as needed

- Serve as liaison to community services (e.g., juvenile justice system, child protective, domestic violence, and mental health services, substance abuse)

- Monitor campus safety and ensure physical safety measures are enforced (e.g., doors/gates locked, parking lot monitoring, etc.)

- Help provide security for potentially contentious parent meetings

- Address community violence that can impact school safety

All of these activities help to prevent violence proactively. In addition, individuals are more likely to report concerns to SROs when positive and trusting relationships have been established upon proactive, not punitive, interactions. For example, the state of New Jersey has implemented the "Handle with Care" program. This program allows law enforcement to share general information with school administrators when a student has experienced an adverse situation in the home (i.e., parent was arrested for domestic violence). This allows administrators to be more trauma-sensitive and proactively provide additional supports for the student.

Case Study (Skylar)

As Drew is scrolling through Instagram posts, one picture immediately stands out. There are guns laying on a bed with a post that states, "*Eastern High School better be prepared as the end is very near.*" Drew notices the post is from Skylar, a student in Drew's 9th grade English class. Drew immediately shows the post to the assistance principal, who assembles the core BTAM team. The school counselor quickly touches base with Skylar's teachers who express concerns regarding recent escalating behaviors, increased anger, a decrease in academic performance, and themes of violence in written assignments. They also mention that Skylar seems to lack empathy for others and likes to be in control. When Skylar's teachers expressed their concerns, Skylar told them they were overreacting and "not to worry as all will be good." The teachers had referred Skylar to the behavioral intervention team and he was to be discussed at their next meeting. The school psychologist tried to find Skylar to initiate a conversation about the reported concerns, but Skylar is absent. Simultaneously, the SRO and technology specialist are looking into the social media, school email, and the internet search histories Skylar conducted using school-issued platforms and devices. Multiple references to previous mass shootings are discovered along with a picture posted an hour ago showing Skylar holding a gun and pointing it at the school's yearbook lying on a bed next to more guns. The core BTAM team, SRO, and local law enforcement immediately collaborate to determine Skylar's current whereabouts. The school counselor contacts parents and discrete actions are taken to ensure school grounds are secure.

QUESTIONS to CONSIDER

1. How engaged in the BTAM process is the administrator at your school(s)? Is there a need to increase engagement?

2. What alternatives to suspension could be used in your school(s)?

3. What is the role of the SRO in the BTAM process at your school(s)?

KEY POINTS

- Administrators must engage and play a key leadership role in BTAM.

- Administrators set the climate and culture for the school, and they set the tone of whether the BTAM is collaborative or adversarial.

- Consequences must be implemented with care and alternatives to suspension must be utilized.

- School mental health professionals and SROs need to be engaged in prevention and intervention activities.

- SROs should not be engaged in school discipline unless absolutely necessary to ensure physical safety.

9

Role of School Mental Health Professionals

School psychologists, school counselors, and school social workers play a key role in the BTAM process. In addition to serving on the core team and being engaged in the entire assessment process, they also play a key role in prevention, intervention, and management.

Prevention (Universal—Tier 1 Interventions)

School mental health professionals (SMHP) are adept at establishing trusting and collaborative relationships with students, staff, and parents. This increases reporting and the ability to proactively address emerging concerns. Because they serve the entire school, they also have a good understanding of the climate and culture, as well as intra- and interpersonal dynamics. Their engagement in universal prevention programming is key.

Specific involvement can include:

- Engaging in resource mapping, including conducting a needs assessment and gap analysis regarding academics, social-emotional, and safety programming

- Planning and coordination of academic, school climate, and behavioral/mental health screenings

- Effective data-based decision-making using resource mapping, screening, academic and behavioral data

- Serving on school safety/crisis teams to inform comprehensive safety initiatives and crisis prevention, intervention, and recovery

- Facilitating parent-school collaboration (e.g., monthly parent newsletter articles, back-to-school nights to highlight social-emotional supports, mental health awareness initiatives, etc.)

- Facilitating the implementation of universal prevention programs (e.g., suicide and bullying prevention, positive behavior supports, social media responsibility, mentoring, peer mediation)

- Facilitating the integration of mental health and BTAM awareness training into health, SEL, and/or academic curricula; teaching awareness trainings

- Identifying and addressing potential barriers to reporting

- Teaching emotional regulation strategies (e.g., mindfulness, yoga, conflict resolution)

- Facilitating additional faculty training:

  o Trauma-informed/sensitive approach for increased understanding of how trauma impacts behavior, emotional regulation, and academic achievement

  o PFA (psychological first aid)/MHFA (mental health first aid)

  o De-escalation training

Targeted Intervention (Tier 2 Interventions)

School mental health professionals can also help to teach replacement skills by engaging in the delivery of or referring the student to receive Tier 2 supports. Specific involvement at the Tier 2 level can include:

- Individual and/or small group interventions that focus on academic skills, learning, socialization, mental health, and emotional regulation (e.g., anger or anxiety management)

- Increased social supports and build positive relationships (e.g., lunch bunch, peer and adult mentoring programs)

- Teaching small groups SEL lessons

- Conducting functional behavioral assessment (FBA; note— FBAs *can* be conducted with general education students and as part of the BTAM process)

- Developing behavioral intervention plan (BIP)

- Implementing behavior modification interventions

- Conducting suicide risk assessment

- Referring to school intervention teams (e.g., academic/ behavior intervention team)

- Serving on school intervention/problem solving teams

- Developing progress monitoring plans to objectively measure change over time

- Collaborating with students and parents in a nonconfrontational manner; educating them about positive outcomes that can result from BTAM assessment

- Coordinating with community providers

Intensive Intervention and Management (Tier 3 Interventions)

School mental health professionals are best suited to recognize when a referral to more intensive services (e.g., special education, mental health treatment) is needed. In addition, if the person of concern is hospitalized, the school mental health professional can identify and provide relevant information to hospital personnel (with appropriate releases of information signed or utilization of FERPA/HIPAA exceptions to confidentiality). Referral for more intensive services can be a key component to the long-term management of risk and improved well-being. It is important to reiterate that a referral to special education may not be appropriate. However, if the individual qualifies for services, ongoing engagement in their programming is critical for progress monitoring. If outside services are being received, coordination with school personnel is critical to reinforcing skill sets being learned and ensuring continuity of services.

Specific involvement at the Tier 3 level can also include:

- Facilitating simultaneous engagement in Tier 1 and Tier 2 interventions

- Providing individual counseling

- Helping to develop and/or progress monitor the intensive monitoring and supervision plan

- Helping to develop and monitor effectiveness of the behavioral intervention plan (BIP)

- Facilitating the delivery of intensive/alternative educational programming

- Facilitating the student's reintegration into general education setting when appropriate progress is made or behavioral consequences have concluded (e.g., suspension, expulsion)

  o Ensure supports are engaged to help facilitate the student who is returning.

  o If other students are hesitant for the student of concern to return, then individual, small-group, or classroom discussions to address these concerns may need to be conducted, with an emphasis on importance of supporting each other in making positive changes.

Two important notes:

1. A student *can* receive counseling services by school mental health personnel and community ("outside") mental health providers concurrently. There are false misperceptions that they cannot co-occur. We do not stop teaching reading when parents hire a reading tutor. Receiving both services in-school and "outside" therapy can facilitate positive growth, particularly when parents sign the release of information (ROI) to allow for coordination between professionals. If the BTAM process is seen as supportive, most parents are willing to sign the ROI.

2. There is often the assumption that reintegration back into the general education setting must be the goal. Some students feel more comfortable in smaller/alternative education settings. If reintegration is forced upon them, they may escalate behaviors in order to avoid reintegration. These dynamics must be recognized, validated, and addressed to avoid escalation.

Case Study (Jordan)

The school psychologist, counselor, and social worker were very involved in providing Tier 1, 2 and 3 supports for Jordan. The school psychologist provided 1:1 counseling supports, integrating social-emotion regulation and coping strategies. The school counselor checked in daily with Jordan and attended Jordan's student intervention team meetings to review progress monitoring data and to ensure the BTAM management plan was effective. The school social worker engaged wraparound community supports for Jordan's family, including financial and substance abuse counseling for the mother and additional mental health supports for Jordan. Teachers were also provided additional strategies on how to meet Jordan's academic and social-emotional needs. This gave Jordan hope, and the supports were very effective in helping to control frustrations with others and engage with positive adults and peers. Due to ongoing stressors, the management plan continues to remain in place. Jordan is responding well, and no escalation of behaviors has been observed.

The school administrators and mental health staff reviewed the survey data and discovered that many students were experiencing signs of anxiety, sadness, and uncertainty. SEL lessons were integrated into advisory groups and the health curriculum to facilitate adapting coping strategies. Advisory group discussions were also held to discuss the importance of not spreading false information.

Case Study (Blake)

The school psychologist and the special education team reviewed Blake's behavior plan. They made adjustments to specifically add in prompts before transition times, identified a cool-down place in the classroom Blake for go to when overwhelmed or frustrated (instead of running out of the room), and provided directive statements in a neutral (not demanding) voice. Blake's parents also agreed to use similar strategies at home, and a reinforcement system was established to reward Blake he used replacement skills.

QUESTIONS to CONSIDER

1. How can school mental health professionals increase the amount of time spent in delivering interventions?

2. What are the barriers to school mental health professionals expanding their roles?

KEY POINTS

- SMHP should be engaged in Tier 1, 2, and 3 supports.
- The expertise of SMHP personnel should be utilized in developing prevention programs and to help provide interventions.
- Collaboration between SMHP and community support providers is critical to continuity of services.
- SMHP can and should provide mental health supports in schools.

Community Partnerships and Transitioning to the Adult Community

Community partnerships are often critical to help with the management of concerns. However, it is important to acknowledge that community resources can be hard to find. Below is an overview of community resources that can support the BTAM management. Please note that this is not an exhaustive list. You will want to find out what is available in your area.

Community Activities

Increasing engagement in prosocial activities helps facilitate positive connections.

- Mentoring programs
- Boys and Girls Club
- YMCA
- Sports
- Drama and art clubs
- Leadership programs
- Skill-based programs (culinary, automotive, computer science, etc.)
- Volunteer activities
- Youth groups
- Enrichment programs
- Summer programs

Community Resources

- Mental health resources
- Housing
- Food
- Domestic violence

- Parenting classes
- Substance abuse
- Diversion programs
- Employment/job readiness

Academic Resources

- Community college
- Technical/trade schools
- University counseling center
- Tutoring
- Academic advisor

- Programs through academic/ disability support center (i.e., program for those on the autism spectrum; LD supports)
- Careful selection of academic programming

Community Threat Assessment Teams

For those students who will be graduating or have been expelled, pathway behaviors and ongoing stressors may still be a concern. They are losing the familiarity of the K-12 setting, they are now disengaged from supports and peers, and they lose their familiar structure and routine. Transitioning from the K-12 environment to the community environment can escalate stressors and losses. These students need hope for the future and need to know people care. One school district has made it a point to follow up monthly with their high-risk threat assessment cases even after graduation. This has been a huge success. Some of these young adults engaged in higher education opportunities. Some experienced subsequent stressors for which the K-12 team was able to help engage community supports. Others enrolled in trade schools, and others found employment. After two years, none of them has made subsequent threats, and the monthly check-ins have been critical to keeping supports engaged.

If there is a community threat assessment team, it is important to consider making a referral to this team when graduation is approaching. Ongoing engagements and supports can prevent escalation and help the individual onto a more positive pathway. Check with your local law enforcement agency, community mental health agencies, and/or social service agency about continuity of supports. Some cities/counties have established multi-disciplinary community threat assessment teams with a school district representative as a member of the community team. Community teams often include representation from the following members: local, county, and state police; local and state courts; district attorney's office; school district/educational services centers; health department; and social services. This representation allows for greater coordination of interventions and management supports. The Salem-Keizer Threat Assessment System provides guidance on how to build a community team: http://www.studentthreatassessment.org/home.

Case Study (Jordan)

Jordan will graduate in May and still has hopes of attending community college. The school counselor is working with Jordan to secure financial aid, grants, and scholarships. Community counseling supports will continue to work with Jordan after graduation, and the campus counseling clinic will also serve as a resource. Engagement in campus activity groups will also be explored, along with summer employment. The SRO will also continue to mentor Jordan and provide weekly summer check-ins.

QUESTIONS to CONSIDER

1. What community resources are available?

2. How can collaboration between school and community resources be improved?

3. How can students be better supported with transitions like graduation?

KEY POINTS

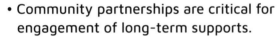

- Community partnerships are critical for engagement of long-term supports.
- Engage a community BTAM team (if one is available) for ongoing progress monitoring and supports beyond a student's graduation.
- Supports help to mitigate escalation.

CONCLUDING THOUGHTS

Our students need our guidance and supports now more than ever before. While some students have a legitimate intent to harm, most concerning behaviors are a cry for help. You might just be that one person who helps a student onto a more positive pathway. Literally and figuratively, you may be saving their life and the lives of others—including your own.

Juggling the multiple demands in education these days is exhausting. While BTAM may feel like "one more thing to do," engage the team approach. You cannot and should not do this alone. High-quality, objective team decisions based upon known facts help to ensure fair, equitable, and positive outcomes. The impact of biases and systemic discriminatory practices must be recognized and addressed. Professionals involved in BTAM need to respect the power they have in making decisions that can significantly impact someone's future.

And remember...You may never know if you prevented a crisis, but you will know if you didn't. Interventions and supports matter!

DOWNLOADABLE RESOURCES

The resources in this book are available for you
as a digital download!

Please visit **15minutefocusseries.com** and click this book
cover on the page. Once you've clicked the book cover,
a prompt will ask you for a code to unlock the activities.

Please enter code:

Threat335

Resources and Training

Threat Assessment Models for K-12 Schools

Secret Service Model:

- *Enhancing School Safety Using a Threat Assessment Model: An Operational Guide for Preventing Targeted School Violence* (2018)
  https://www.cisa.gov/publication/enhancing-school-safety-using-threat-assessment-model-operational-guide-preventing
- *Making Prevention a Reality: Identifying, Assessing & Managing the Threat of Targeted Attacks* (2017)
  www.fbi.gov/file-repository/making-prevention-a-reality.pdf
- *The Final Report and Findings of the Safe School Initiative: Implications for the Prevention of School Attacks in the United States* (2004)
  https://www2.ed.gov/admins/lead/safety/preventingattacksreport.pdf
- *Threat Assessment in Schools: A Guide to Managing Threatening Situations and to Creating Safe School Climates* (2004)
  https://www2.ed.gov/admins/lead/safety/threatassessmentguide.pdf

Salem-Kaiser System (student and adult/community teams):

- http://www.studentthreatassessment.org/home

Comprehensive School Threat Assessment Guidelines (C-STAG):

- https://education.virginia.edu/faculty-research/centers-labs-projects/research-labs/youth-violence-project/comprehensive-school

Additional Resources for K-12 Training and Implementation

SIGMA Threat Management Associates

- http://www.sigmatma.com/k-12-schools/

Virginia Department of Criminal Justice Services

- https://www.dcjs.virginia.gov/virginia-center-school-and-campus-safety/threat-assessment-virginia

Colorado School Safety Resource Center

- https://www.colorado.gov/pacific/cssrc/threat-assessment

Wisconsin Department of Justice

- https://www.doj.state.wi.us/office-school-safety/resources

Additional Threat Assessment Resources

Protecting America's Schools: A U.S. Secret Service Analysis of Targeted School Violence (2019)

- https://www.schoolsafety.gov/resource/protecting-americas-schools-us-secret-service-analysis-targeted-school-violence

Guide for Developing High-Quality School Emergency Plans (2013)

- https://rems.ed.gov/docs/rems_ihe_guide_508.pdf

Role of Districts in Developing High-Quality School Emergency Operations Plans
- https://rems.ed.gov/DistrictGuide.aspx

National School Boards Association (2018). Fostering Safer Schools: A Legal Guide for School Board Members on School Safety

- https://www.nsba.org/-/media/NSBA/File/legal-fostering-safe-schools-guide.pdf

Arapahoe High School post incident reports

- https://cssrc.colorado.gov/claire-davis-school-safety-act

Marjory Stoneman Douglas High School Public Safety Commission

- http://www.fdle.state.fl.us/msdhs/commissionreport.pdf
- http://www.fdle.state.fl.us/MSDHS/MSD-Report-2-Public-Version.pdf
- https://efactssc-public.flcourts.org/casedocuments/2019/240/2019-240_miscdoc_365089_e20.pdf

Sandy Hook Advisory Commission Report

- https://www.nctsn.org/resources/final-report-of-the-sandy-hook-advisory-commission

Information Sharing Resources

FERPA

- https://www2.ed.gov/policy/gen/guid/fpco/ferpa/index.html
- http://rems.ed.gov/K12FERPA.aspx
- https://studentprivacy.ed.gov/faq/does-ferpa-permit-sharing-education-records-outside-law-enforcement-officials-mental-health

U.S. Department of Education (2019). "School Resource Officers, Law Enforcement Units, and the Family Educational Rights and Privacy Act (FERPA)"

- https://studentprivacy.ed.gov/resources/school-resource-officers-school-law-enforcement-units-and-ferpa

HIPAA: https://www.hhs.gov/hipaa/index.html

Additional School Safety Resources

National Association of School Psychologists

BTAM Best Practice Considerations, BTAM in the Virtual Environment, & Conducting Suicide Risk Assessments in the Virtual Environment (also found in downloadable resources)

- https://www.nasponline.org/resources-and-publications/resources-and-podcasts/covid-19-resource-center/crisis-and-mental-health-resources

General Crisis Resources

- https://www.nasponline.org/resources-and-publications/resources-and-podcasts

Framework for Safe & Successful Schools (also found in downloadable resources)

- https://www.nasponline.org/resources-and-publications/resources-and-podcasts/school-climate-safety-and-crisis/systems-level-prevention/a-framework-for-safe-and-successful-schools

PREPaRE School Crisis Prevention & Intervention Training Curriculum

- https://www.nasponline.org/professional-development/prepare-training-curriculum

National Association of School Resource Officers

To Protect and Educate: The School Resource Officer and the Prevention of Violence in Schools

- https://www.nasro.org/clientuploads/About-Mission/NASRO-To-Protect-and-Educate-nosecurity.pdf

NASRO Position Statement on Police Involvement in Student Discipline

- https://www.nasro.org/aboutnasro/nasro-position-statement-on-police-involvement-in-student-discipline/

Standards and Best Practices for School Resource Officer Programs

- https://www.nasro.org/clientuploads/About-Mission/NASRO-Standards-and-Best-Practices.pdf

Safe and Sound Schools – School Safety Resources and Staff Development

- https://www.safeandsoundschools.org/

Safer Schools Together – Digital Threat Assessment Training

- https://saferschoolstogether.com/

Collaborative for Academic, Social, and Emotional Learning

- www.casel.org

Positive Behavior Supports

- https://www.pbis.org/

Reporting App/Tip Hotline:
Legal & Financial Considerations

Questions to consider before any app/tip line is adopted:

1. Are there enough operators to receive the volume of calls/texts/reports?

2. Is there enough funding (state or federal) for adequate staffing of the local personnel (law enforcement, emergency management, 911 operators, school personnel, etc.) necessary to oversee this application responsibly? If so, what are the sources of funding?

   • Is there sufficient funding to accommodate the additional resources needed to implement the application?

   • Has a needs-assessment been conducted to determine the necessary funding/resources to implement district/statewide? If so, what are the results?

3. What is the protocol for the anonymity of the "anonymous" caller? When the child calling is a minor, are the parents informed? If so, how, by whom, and when? If not, why not? What are the parents' rights when their minor child reports a tip through the application?

4. Once the tip is received by the call center, what are the security protocols to protect the confidentiality of any student's records, whether school records, disability/medical records, or prior criminal records?

5. What are the exact measures of student privacy and the security of student data upon receipt of a student's call to the call center? Who has access to this data? Security details need to be explained to parents, students, and staff.

6. If district/statewide implementation is rolled out in counties/school systems that do not have adequate staffing, how will calls/tips at the local level be handled if no one staffs this position? Will staff at the Department of Education/Public Instruction, Departments of Public Safety or Juvenile Justice, Attorney General's Office, or any other state agency be

responsible for forecasting, assessing, and helping with these shortfalls that currently exist?

7. For those counties/school systems that have adequate capacity, who will pay the personnel to work beyond their work hours (nights and weekends)?
   - What labor laws are implicated here?
   - Counties and school systems cannot typically require employees to download an application for work purposes on their personal phones. School systems do not pay for phones for many of the personnel who would be expected/required to receive calls/notices through the application. Where are the funds to purchase work phones for these employees in order for them to oversee this application?
   - Are employees expected to download this application on their personal phones and work on nights and weekends receiving triage calls/notices without commensurate pay?
   - What are the liability issues for school personnel/county personnel and school systems/counties overseeing the application? How does this impact confidentiality of records or ability to subpoena personal phones used to receive reports?

8. Where in the law is there immunity (governmental, official, and individual) for allegations of negligence regarding the use of this application?
   - Will the district (or State Department of Education/Public Instruction or State Board of Education) bear the risk and liability for this application?
   - If so, is there adequate insurance or other liability coverage?

Management Considerations

Below is a list of interventions and supports to consider. This is not an exhaustive list but provides guidance as to the multiple options to be considered.

MONITORING		
✓ Check-in, checkout program ✓ Reinforcement program ✓ Safety contract ✓ Adult/increased monitoring ✓ Late arrival/early dismissal ✓ Adult escorts from class to class ✓ Modify daily schedule (reduce free, unsupervised time; travel card). ✓ Restrictions to schedule or activities	✓ Ongoing progress monitoring ✓ Track attendance ✓ Parent-school collaboration ✓ Parent/guardian will increase supervision ✓ Monitor for precipitating events (i.e., anniversaries, losses, perceived injustice, etc.) ✓ Change class schedule	✓ Home visits (check for weapons, etc.) ✓ Searches ✓ Ankle monitor ✓ Ongoing collaboration with agency supports, probation/ juvenile diversion, mental health professionals ✓ Detained, incarcerated, or placed under intensive supervision
RELATIONSHIP BUILDING		
✓ Establish system for student to proactively seek support ✓ Peer mentor ✓ Adult mentor ✓ Provide feedback and mentoring	✓ Peer supports ✓ Increase engagement in school activities ✓ Increase engagement in community activities ✓ Engage in leadership activities	✓ De-escalation training for staff ✓ Monitor reactions to grievances and precipitating events, and provide supports. ✓ Trauma-informed training for staff
SKILL DEVELOPMENT/RESILIENCY BUILDING		
✓ Academic supports ✓ Conflict resolution ✓ Anger management group ✓ Social skills group ✓ Social-emotional learning curriculum	✓ Participation in school activities/clubs ✓ Counseling—in school ✓ Counseling—outside of school ✓ Family supports/ resources	✓ Conduct functional behavioral assessment (FBA) ✓ Develop behavioral intervention plan (BIP). ✓ Supports from behavior specialist/school psychologist

DISCIPLINE

✓ Letter of apology ✓ Conflict resolution ✓ Confrontation/warning ✓ Restorative practice ✓ Removing privileges ✓ Time-out/self-initiated time-out ✓ Behavior contract ✓ Parent meeting	✓ Detention ✓ Alternative to suspension ✓ In-school suspension ✓ Out-of-school suspension ✓ Habitually Disruptive Plan ✓ Alternative placement ✓ Expulsion ✓ Diversion program	✓ Ticketed by law enforcement ✓ Charges filed by law enforcement ✓ Law enforcement diversion program ✓ Court issued non-contact/ protective orders

SCHOOL CLIMATE & CULTURE

✓ Address systemic, procedural, or policy problems that may be precipitating stressors(s)
✓ Build a caring and supportive climate and culture
✓ Implement effective threat and suicide assessment procedures
✓ Universal screenings for academic and social-emotional barriers to learning
	✓ Enhanced social-emotional learning to include:
	  • Bullying prevention
	  • Violence prevention
	  • Suicide prevention
	  • Emotional regulation
	  • Conflict management
	✓ Ensure positive dynamics among staff (serves as modeling for students)
		✓ Early intervention with emerging problems (MTSS supports)
		✓ Explicitly teach about confidential reporting procedures
		✓ Give permission to "Break the Code of Silence" and get help for self/peer who is struggling

References

Amman, M., Bowlin, M., Buckles, L., Burton, K. C., Brunell, K. F., Gibson, K. A., & Robins, C. J. (2017). *Making prevention a reality: Identifying, assessing, and managing the threat of targeted attacks. US Department of Justice.* Accessed March 3, 32021, https://www.fbi.gov/file-repository/making-prevention-a-reality.pdf/view

Centers for Disease Control (CDC) (2020). *Indicators of anxiety or depression based on reported frequency of symptoms during the last 7 days.* Household Pulse Survey. Atlanta, GA: US Department of Health and Human Services, CDC, National Center for Health Statistics. Accessed March 5, 2021, https://www.cdc.gov/nchs/covid19/pulse/mental-health.htm

Cornell, D., Sheras, P., Kaplan, S., McConville, D., Douglass, J., Elkon, A., McKnight, L., Branson, C., & Cole, J. (2004). Guidelines for student threat assessment: Field-test findings. *School Psychology Review*, 33(4), 527–546. Accessed March 1, 2021, https://www.tandfonline.com/doi/abs/10.1080/02796015.2004.12086266

Cornell, D. G., Allen, K., & Fan, X. (2012). A randomized control study of the Virginia Student Threat Assessment Guidelines in kindergarten through grade 12. *School Psychology Review*, 41(1), 100–115. Accessed March 5, 2021, https://www.tandfonline.com/doi/abs/10.1080/02796015.2012.12087378.

Cornell, D., Maeng, J., Huang, F, & Shukla, K., & Konold, T. (2018). Racial/ethnic parity in disciplinary consequences using student threat assessment. *School Psychology Review*, 47(2), 183–195. Accessed February 27, 2021, https://eric.ed.gov/?id=EJ1182056.

Cowan, K. C., Vaillancourt, K., Rossen, E., & Pollitt, K. (2013). *A framework for safe and successful schools* [Brief]. National Association of School Psychologists. Accessed March 3, 2021, https://www.nasponline.org/resources-andpublications/resources/school-safety-and-crisis/a-framework-for-safe-and-successful-schools.

Curtin, SC (2020). *State suicide rates among adolescents and young adults aged 10–24: United States, 2000–2018.* National Vital Statistics Reports; vol 69 no 11. Hyattsville, MD: National Center for Health Statistics. Accessed March 5, 2021, https://www.cdc.gov/nchs/data/nvsr/nvsr69/nvsr-69-11-508.pdf.

Czeisler MÉ, Lane RI, Petrosky E, et al. *Mental Health, Substance Use, and Suicidal Ideation During the COVID-19 Pandemic—United States, June 24–30, 2020.* MMWR Morb Mortal Wkly Rep 2020;69:1049–1057. Accessed March 5, 2021, https://www.cdc.gov/mmwr/volumes/69/wr/mm6932a1.htm.

de Becker, G (1997). *The Gift of Fear and Other Survival Signals That Protect Us From Violence.* New York: Dell Publishing.

Erbacher, T. & Wycoff, K (2021). *A tale of two-pandemics: Equitable and trauma-informed threat assessment processes.* NASP Communiqué, Jan/Feb 2021, 49(5).

Family Educational Rights and Privacy Act of 1974 (FERPA), 20 U.S.C. § 1232g. U.S. Department of Education. Accessed March 9, 2021, https://www2.ed.gov/policy/gen/guid/fpco/ferpa/index.html

Fein, R., Vossekuil, B., Pollack, W., Borum, R., Modzeleski, W., & Reddy, M. (2004). "Threat assessment in schools: A guide to managing threatening situations and to creating safe school climates." US Secret Service and US Department of Education. Accessed March 9, 2021, https://www2.ed.gov/admins/lead/safety/threatassessmentguide.pdf

Hirschfield, P. (2018) Schools and Crime. *Annual Review of Criminology*, 1(1), 149-169. Accessed March 9, 2021, https://www.annualreviews.org/doi/abs/10.1146/annurev-criminol-032317-092358

Langman, P. (2009). *Why Kids Kill: Inside the Minds of School Shooters.* London: Palgrave Macmillan.

Langman, P. (2015). *School Shooters: Understanding High School, College, and Adult Perpetrators.* Lanham: Rowman and Littlefield.

Margolius, M., Doyle Lynch, A., Pufall Jones, E. & Hynes, M. (2020). *The state of Young People during COVID-19: Findings from a nationally representative survey of high school youth.* America's Promise Alliance. Accessed March 5, 2021, https://www.americaspromise.org/resource/state-young-people-during-covid-19

Meloy, J. R., Hoffmann, J., Guldimann, A., & James, D. (2011). The role of warning behaviors in threat assessment: An exploration and suggested typology. *Behavior Sciences and the Law*, 30, 256–279. Accessed February, 27, 2021, https://pubmed.ncbi.nlm.nih.gov/22556034/

Meloy, J. R., Hoffmann, J., Roshdi, K., & Guldimann, A. (2014). Some warning behaviors discriminate between school shooters and other students of concern. *Journal of Threat Assessment and Management*, 1(3), 203–211. Accessed February 25, 2021, http://drreidmeloy.com/wp-content/uploads/2015/12/2014_SomeWarningBeh.pdf

Meloy, J. R., Mohandie, K., Knoll, J., & Hoffmann, J. (2015). The concept of identification in threat assessment. *Behavior Sciences and the Law,* 33, 213–223. Accessed February 15, 2021, https://www.researchgate.net/publication/272890524_The_Concept_of_Identification_in_Threat_Assessment

National Institute of Mental Health (2018). *Suicide.* Accessed March 5, 2021. https://www.nimh.nih.gov/health/statistics/suicide.shtml

National Threat Assessment Center. (2018). *Enhancing school safety using a threat assessment model: An operational guide for preventing targeted school violence.* US Secret Service and Department of Homeland Security. https://www.cisa.gov/publication/enhancing-school-safety-using-threat-assessment-model-operational-guide-preventing

National Threat Assessment Center. (2019). *Protecting America's schools: A U.S. Secret Service analysis of targeted school violence.* US Secret Service and Department of Homeland Security. https://www.secretservice.gov/node/2565

Nicoletti, J., & Spencer-Thomas, S. (2002). *Violence Goes to School.* Bloomington: Solution Tree Press.

Reeves, M. A. L., & Brock, S. E. (2018). School behavioral threat assessment and management. *Contemporary School Psychology,* 22(2). 148–162. Accessed March 1, 2021, https://www.researchgate.net/publication/320216394_School_Behavioral_Threat_Assessment_and_Management

Reeves, M. (2019, updated 2020). *School-based behavioral threat assessment and management: Best practices guide for South Carolina K-12 schools.* South Carolina Department of Education. Accessed February 1, 2021, https://ed.sc.gov/districts-schools/school-safety/resources-and-training/safety-resources/sc-school-based-threat-assessment-guide/

Rosenbaum, J. (2018). Educational and criminal justice outcomes 12 years after school suspension, *Youth and Society,* 52(4), 515-547. Accessed March 2, 2021, https://journals.sagepub.com/doi/abs/10.1177/0044118X17752208

SIGMA Threat Management Associates, LLC. (May 2017). *Integrated threat management: A collaborative approach to identifying, assessing & managing threatening behaviors.* Workshop presented to Maryland Center for School Safety, Annapolis, MD.

U.S. Department of Education. (2013). *Guide for developing high-quality school emergency operations plans.* Author. Accessed March 5, 2021, http://rems.ed.gov/docs/REMS_K-12_Guide_508.pdf

U.S. Department of Education (2019). "School Resource Officers, Law Enforcement Units, and the Family Educational Rights and Privacy Act (FERPA)" Retrieved March 7, 2021, https://studentprivacy.ed.gov/resources/school-resource-officers-school-law-enforcement-units-and-ferpa

U.S. Department of Education. (2007). *Balancing student privacy and school safety: A guide to the Family Educational Rights and Privacy Act (FERPA) for elementary and secondary schools.* Author. Accessed March 24, 2021, https://studentprivacy.ed.gov/?src=rn

U.S. Departments of Education, Justice, Homeland Security, & Health and Human Services. (2018). *Final report of the federal commission on school safety.* Accessed March 5, 2021, https://www2.ed.gov/documents/school-safety/school-safety-report.pdf?utm

U.S. Department of Justice and FBI. (2014). *A study of active shooter incidents in the United States between 2000 and 2013.* Accessed on March 5, 2021, https://www.fbi.gov/file-repository/active-shooter-study-2000-2013-1.pdf/view

Virginia Center for School & Campus Safety. (2016). *Threat assessment in Virginia schools: Model policies procedures and guidelines.* Accessed March 1, 2021, https://www.dcjs.virginia.gov/sites/dcjs.virginia.gov/files/publications/law-enforcement/threat-assessment-model-policies-procedures-and-guidelinespdf.pdf

Vossekuil, B., Reddy, M., Fein, R., Borum, R., & Modzeleski, W. (2002). *The final report and findings of the safe school initiative: Implications for the prevention of school attacks in the United States.* US Secret Service and US Department of Education. Accessed March 3, 2021, http://www.nccpsafety.org/assets/files/library/Prevention_of_School_Attacks.pdf

Endnotes

1 A. Margolius, et. al., "State of young people during COVID-19."

2 National Institute of Mental Health, "Suicide."

3 S.C. Curtin, "State suicide rates."

4 Centers for Disease Control (CDC), "Anxiety and Depression."

5 M. E. Czeisler, et al. "Mental Health, Substance Use."

6 B. Vossekuil, et. al, "The final report and findings of the safe school initiative."

7 U.S. Department of Justice and FBI, "A study of active shooter incidents."

8 B. Vossekuil, et al, "The final report and findings of the safe school initiative."

9 M. Amman, et. al, "Making prevention a reality."

10 U.S. Department of Education, "Final report on school safety."

11 D.G. Cornell, et. al., "Virginia Student Threat Assessment Guidelines."

12 D. Cornell, et. al., "Racial/ethnic parity in disciplinary consequences."

13 R. Fein, et. al., "Threat assessment in schools."

14 National Threat Assessment Center, "Enhancing school safety."

15 At time of publication, the establishment of K-12 BTAM team is required by law for schools in Virginia, Maryland, Florida, Illinois, Texas, Rhode Island, Tennessee, Oregon, South Carolina, Kentucky, Minnesota, Ohio, and Washington. Georgia requires training. However, this list may not be exhaustive as many states also have legislation under consideration.

16 U.S. Department of Education, "Protecting student privacy."

17 K.C. Cowan, et. al., "A framework for safe and successful schools."

18 J. A. Durlak and J. L. Mahoney, "Practical benefits of an SEL program."

19 D. Cornell, et. al., "Guidelines for student threat assessment."

20 https://safe2tell.org

21 U.S. Department of Education, "School Resource Officers."

22 National Threat Assessment Center, "Protecting America's schools."

23 T. Erbacher and K. Wycoff, "A tale of two-pandemics."

24 J. Nicoletti and S. Spencer-Thomas, Violence Goes to School.

25 Galvin de Becker, The Gift of Fear.

26 Amman, et. al., "Making prevention a reality."

27 National Threat Assessment Center, "Protecting America's schools."

28 Nora Gordon. "Disproportionality in student discipline: Connecting policy to research." The Brookings Institution. January 18, 2018. https://www.brookings.edu/research/disproportionality-in-student-discipline-connecting-policy-to-research/.

29 P. Hirschfield, "Schools and Crime."

30 "Training Courses," National Association of School Resource Officers, https://www.nasro.org/training/training-courses/

31 "NASRO position statement on police involvement student discipline," National Association of School Resources Officers. August 14, 2015. https://www.nasro.org/news/2015/04/14/news-releases/nasro-position-statement-on-police-involvement-in-student-discipline/.